desamparados →

YOGA

as Philosophy and Religion

Surendranath Dasgupta

For Natty,
Enjoy; hope it's
good...
Mush

DOVER PUBLICATIONS, INC.
Mineola, New York

AS A HUMBLE TOKEN

OF DEEPEST REGARD AND GRATEFULNESS

TO THE

MAHARAJA SIR MANINDRACHANDRA NUNDY

K.C.I.E.

WHOSE NOBLE CHARACTER AND SELF-DENYING CHARITIES

HAVE ENDEARED HIM TO THE PEOPLE OF BENGAL

AND

WHO SO KINDLY OFFERED ME HIS WHOLE-HEARTED

PATRONAGE IN

ENCOURAGING MY ZEAL FOR LEARNING AT A TIME

WHEN I WAS IN SO GREAT A NEED OF IT

Bibliographical Note

This Dover edition, first published in 2002, is an unabridged republication of the work originally published by Kegan Paul, Trench, Trubner & Co., Ltd., London, and E. P. Dutton & Co., New York, 1924.

Library of Congress Cataloging-in-Publication Data

Dasagupta, Surendranath, 1885-1952.
Yoga as philosophy and religion / Surendranath Dasgupta.
p. cm.
Originally published: London : K. Paul, Trench, Trubner & Co. ; New York: E.P. Dutton, 1924.
Includes index.
ISBN 0-486-42505-3 (pbk.)
1. Yoga. 2. Philosophy, Hindu. 3. Pataäjali. I. Title.

B132.Y6 D27 2002
181'.45—dc21

2002074160

Manufactured in the United States of America
Dover Publications, Inc., 31 East 2nd Street, Mineola, N.Y. 11501

PREFACE

THIS little volume is an attempt at a brief exposition of the philosophical and religious doctrines found in Patañjali's *Yoga-sūtra* as explained by its successive commentaries of Vyāsa, Vācaspati, Vijñāna Bhikshu, and others. The exact date of Patañjali cannot be definitely ascertained, but if his identity with the other Patañjali, the author of the Great Commentary (*Mahābhāshya*) on Pāṇini's grammar, could be conclusively established, there would be some evidence in our hands that he lived in 150 B.C. I have already discussed this subject in the first volume of my *A History of Indian Philosophy*, where the conclusion to which I arrived was that, while there was some evidence in favour of their identity, there was nothing which could be considered as being conclusively against it. The term Yoga, according to Patañjali's definition, means the final annihilation (*nirodha*) of all the mental states (*cittavṛtti*) involving the preparatory stages in which the mind has to be habituated to being steadied into particular types of graduated mental states. This was actually practised in India for a long time before Patañjali lived; and it is very probable that certain philosophical, psychological, and practical doctrines associated with it were also current long before Patañjali. Patañjali's work is, however, the earliest systematic compilation on the subject that is known to us. It is impossible, at this distance of time, to determine the extent to which Patañjali may claim originality. Had it not been for the labours of the later commentators, much of what is found in Patañjali's aphorisms would have remained extremely obscure and doubtful, at least to all those who were not associated with such ascetics as practised them, and who derived the theoretical and practical knowledge of the subject from their preceptors in an upward succession of generations leading up to the age of Patañjali, or even before him. It is well to bear in mind that Yoga is even now practised in India, and the continuity of traditional instruction handed down from teacher to pupil is not yet completely broken.

If anyone wishes methodically to pursue a course which may lead him ultimately to the goal aimed at by Yoga, he must devote his entire life to it under the strict practical guidance of an advanced teacher. The present work can in no sense be considered as a practical guide for such purposes. But it is also erroneous to think—as many uninformed people do—that the only interest of Yoga lies in its practical side. The philosophical, psychological, cosmological, ethical, and religious doctrines, as well as its doctrines regarding matter and change, are extremely interesting in themselves, and have a definitely assured place in the history of the progress of human thought; and, for a right understanding of the essential features of the higher thoughts of India, as well as of the practical side of Yoga, their knowledge is indispensable.

The Yoga doctrines taught by Patañjali are regarded as the highest of all Yogas (*Rājayoga*), as distinguished from other types of Yoga practices, such as *Haṭhayoga* or *Man-*

trayoga. Of these *Haṭhayoga* consists largely of a system of bodily exercises for warding off diseases, and making the body fit for calmly bearing all sorts of physical privations and physical strains. *Mantrayoga* is a course of meditation on certain mystical syllables which leads to the audition of certain mystical sounds. This book does not deal with any of these mystical practices nor does it lay any stress on the performance of any of those miracles described by Patañjali. The scope of this work is limited to a brief exposition of the intellectual foundation—or the theoretical side—of the Yoga practices, consisting of the philosophical, psychological, cosmological, ethical, religious, and other doctrines which underlie these practices. The affinity of the system of Sāṃkhya thought, generally ascribed to a mythical sage, Kapila, to that of Yoga of Patañjali is so great on most important points of theoretical interest that they may both be regarded as two different modifications of one common system of ideas. I have, therefore, often taken the liberty of explaining Yoga ideas by a reference to kindred ideas in Sāṃkhya. But the doctrines of Yoga could very well have been compared or contrasted with great profit with the doctrines of other systems of Indian thought. This has purposely been omitted here as it has already been done by me in my *Yoga Philosophy in relation to other Systems of Indian Thought*, the publication of which has for long been unavoidably delayed. All that may be expected from the present volume is that it will convey to the reader the essential features of the Yoga system of thought. How far this expectation will be realized from this book it will be for my readers to judge. It is hoped that the chapter on "Kapila and Pātañjala School of Sāṃkhya" in my *A History of Indian Philosophy* (Vol. I. Cambridge University Press, 1922) will also prove helpful for the purpose.

I am deeply indebted to my friend Mr. Douglas Ainslie for the numerous corrections and suggestions regarding the English style that he was pleased to make throughout the body of the manuscript and the very warm encouragement that he gave me for the publication of this work. In this connection I also beg to offer my best thanks for the valuable suggestions which I received from the reviser of the press. Had it not been for these, the imperfections of the book would have been still greater. The quaintness and inelegance of some of my expressions would, however, be explained if it were borne in mind that here, as well as in my *A History of Indian Philosophy*, I have tried to resist the temptation of making the English happy at the risk of sacrificing the approach to exactness of the philosophical sense; and many ideas of Indian philosophy are such that an exact English rendering of them often becomes hopelessly difficult.

I am grateful to my friend and colleague, Mr. D. K. Sen, M.A., for the kind assistance that he rendered in helping me to prepare the index.

Last of all, I must express my deep sense of gratefulness to Sir Ashutosh Mookerjee, Kt., C.S.I., etc. etc., and the University of Calcutta, for kindly permitting me to utilize my *A Study of Patañjali*, which is a Calcutta University publication, for the present work.

S. N. DASGUPTA.

PRESIDENCY COLLEGE, CALCUTTA,
April, 1924.

CONTENTS

BOOK I. YOGA METAPHYSICS:

BOOK II. YOGA ETHICS AND PRACTICE:

YOGA AS PHILOSOPHY AND RELIGION

BOOK I. YOGA METAPHYSICS

CHAPTER I

PRAKṚTI

HOWEVER dogmatic a system of philosophical enquiry may appear to us, it must have been preceded by a criticism of the observed facts of experience. The details of the criticism and the processes of self-argumentation by which the thinker arrived at his theory of the Universe might indeed be suppressed, as being relatively unimportant, but a thoughtful reader would detect them as lying in the background behind the shadow of the general speculations, but at the same time setting them off before our view. An Aristotle or a Patañjali may not make any direct mention of the arguments which led him to a dogmatic assertion of his theories, but for a reader who intends to understand them thoroughly it is absolutely necessary that he should read them in the light as far as possible of the inferred presuppositions and inner arguments of their minds; it is in this way alone that he can put himself in the same line of thinking with the thinker whom he is willing to follow, and can grasp him to the fullest extent. In offering this short study of the Pātañjala metaphysics, I shall therefore try to supplement it with such of my inferences of the presuppositions of Patañjali's mind, which I think will add to the clearness of the exposition of his views, though I am fully alive to the difficulties of making such inferences about a philosopher whose psychological, social, religious and moral environments differed so widely from ours.

An enquiry into the relations of the mental phenomena to the physical has sometimes given the first start to philosophy. The relation of mind to matter is such an important problem of philosophy that the existing philosophical systems may roughly be classified according to the relative importance that has been attached to mind or to matter. There have been chemical, mechanical and biological conceptions which have ignored mind as a separate entity and have dogmatically affirmed it to be the product of matter only.* There have been theories of the other extreme, which have dispensed with matter altogether and have boldly affirmed that matter as such has no reality at all, and that thought is the only thing which can be called Real in the highest sense. All matter as such is non-Being or Māyā or Avidyā. There have been Nihilists like the Śūnyavādi Buddhists who have gone so far as to assert that neither matter nor mind exists. Some have asserted that matter is only thought externalized, some have regarded the principle of matter as the unknowable Thing-in-itself, some have regarded them as separate independent entities held within a higher reality called God, or as two of his attributes only, and some have regarded their difference as being only one of grades of intelligence, one merging slowly and imperceptibly into the other and held together in concord with each other by pre-established harmony.

Underlying the metaphysics of the Yoga system of thought as taught by Patañjali and as elaborated by his commentators we find an acute analysis of matter and thought. Matter

* See Ward's *Naturalism and Agnosticism.*

on the one hand, mind, the senses, and the ego on the other are regarded as nothing more than two different kinds of modifications of one primal cause, the Prakṛti. But the self-intelligent principle called Purusha (spirit) is distinguished from them. Matter consists only of three primal qualities or rather substantive entities, which he calls the Sattva or intelligence-stuff, Rajas or energy, and Tamas—the factor of obstruction or mass or inertia. It is extremely difficult truly to conceive of the nature of these three kinds of entities or Guṇas, as he calls them, when we consider that these three elements alone are regarded as composing all phenomena, mental and physical. In order to comprehend them rightly it will be necessary to grasp thoroughly the exact relation between the mental and the physical. What are the real points of agreement between the two ? How can the same elements be said to behave in one case as the conceiver and in the other case as the conceived ? Thus Vācaspati says :—

" The reals (guṇas) have two forms, viz. the determiner or the perceiver, and the perceived or the determined. In the aspect of the determined or the perceived, the guṇas evolve themselves as the five infra-atomic potentials, the five gross elements and their compounds. In the aspect of perceiver or determiner, they form the modifications of the ego together with the senses.*

It is interesting to notice here the two words used by Vācaspati in characterising the twofold aspect of the guṇa viz. *vyavasāyātmakatva*, their nature as the determiner or perceiver, and *vyavaseyātmakatva*, their nature as determined or perceived. The elements which compose the phenomena of the objects of perception are the same as those which form the phenomena of the perceiving ; their only distinction is that one is the determined and the other is the determiner. What we call the psychosis involving intellection, sensing and

* Vācaspati's *Tattvavaiśāradī* on the *Vyāsa-bhāshya*, III. 47.

the ego, and what may be called the infra-atoms, atoms and their combinations, are but two different types of modifications of the same stuff of reals. There is no intrinsic difference in nature between the mental and the physical.

The mode of causal transformation is explained by Vijñāna Bhikshu in his commentary on the system of Sāṃkhya as if its functions consisted only in making manifest what was already there in an unmanifested form. Thus he says, "just as the image already existing in the stone is only manifested by the activity of the statuary, so the causal activity also generates only that activity by which an effect is manifested as if it happened or came into being at the present moment."* The effects are all always existent, but some of them are sometimes in an unmanifested state. What the causal operation, viz. the energy of the agent and the suitable collocating instruments and conditions, does is to set up an activity by which the effect may be manifested at the present moment.

With Sāṃkhya-Yoga, sattva, rajas and tamas are substantive entities which compose the reality of the mental and the physical.† The mental and the physical represent two different orders of modifications, and one is not in any way superior to the other. As the guṇas conjointly form the mani-

* *Sāṃkhyapravacanabhāshya*, I. 120.

† It is indeed difficult to say what was the earliest conception of the guṇas. But there is reason to believe, as I have said elsewhere, that guṇa in its earliest acceptance meant qualities. It is very probable that as the Sāṃkhya philosophy became more and more systematised it was realised that there was no ultimate distinction between substance and qualities. In consequence of such a view the guṇas which were originally regarded as qualities began to be regarded as substantive entities and no contradiction was felt. Bhikshu in many places describes the guṇas as substantive entities (*dravya*) and their division into three classes as being due to the presence of three kinds of class-characteristics. This would naturally mean that within the same class there were many other differences which have not been taken into account (*Yoga-vārttika*, II. 18). But it cannot be said that the view that the guṇas are substantive entities and that there is no difference between qualities and substances is regarded as a genuine Sāṃkhya view even as early as Śaṅkara. See *Gītābhāshya*, XIV. 5.

fold without, by their varying combinations, as well as all the diverse internal functions, faculties and phenomena, they are in themselves the absolute potentiality of all things, mental and physical. Thus Vyāsa in describing the nature of the knowable, writes: "The nature of the knowable is now described:—The knowable, consisting of the objects of enjoyment and liberation, as the gross elements and the perceptive senses, is characterised by three essential traits—illumination, energy and inertia. The sattva is of the nature of illumination. Rajas is of the nature of energy. Inertia (tamas) is of the nature of inactivity. The guṇa entities with the above characteristics are capable of being modified by mutual influence on one another, by their proximity. They are evolving. They have the characteristics of conjunction and separation. They manifest forms by one lending support to the others by proximity. None of these loses its distinct power into those of the others, even though any one of them may exist as the principal factor of a phenomenon with the others as subsidiary thereto. The guṇas forming the three classes of substantive entities manifest themselves as such by their similar kinds of power. When any one of them plays the rôle of the principal factor of any phenomenon, the others also show their presence in close contact. Their existence as subsidiary energies of the principal factor is inferred by their distinct and independent functioning, even though it be as subsidiary qualities." * The Yoga theory does not acknowledge qualities as being different from substances. The ultimate substantive entities are called guṇas, which as we have seen are of three kinds. The guṇa entities are infinite in number; each has an individual existence, but is always acting in co-operation with others. They may be divided into three classes in accordance with their similarities

* See *Vyāsa-bhāshya* on Patañjali's *Yoga-sūtras*, II. 18, and Vācaspati's *Tattvavaiśāradī* on it.

of behaviour (śīla). Those which behave in the way of intellection are called *sattva*, those which behave in the way of producing effort of movement are called *rajas*, and those which behave differently from these and obstruct their process are called *tamas*. We have spoken above of a primal cause *prakṛti*. But that is not a separate category independent of the guṇas. Prakṛti is but a name for the guṇa entities when they exist in a state of equilibrium. All that exists excepting the purushas are but the guṇa entities in different kinds of combination amongst themselves. The effects they produce are not different from them but it is they themselves which are regarded as causes in one state and effects in another. The difference of combination consists in this, that in some combinations there are more of sattva entities than rajas or tamas, and in others more of rajas or more of tamas. These entities are continually uniting and separating. But though they are thus continually dividing and uniting in new combinations the special behaviour or feature of each class of entities remains ever the same. Whatever may be the nature of any particular combination the sattva entities participating in it will retain their intellective functions, rajas their energy functions, and tamas the obstructing ones. But though they retain their special features in spite of their mutual difference they hold fast to one another in any particular combination (*tulyajātīyātulyajātīyaśaktibhedānupātinaḥ* which Bhikshu explains as *aviśeshenopashṭambhakasvabhāvāḥ*). In any particular combination it is the special features of those entities which predominate that manifest themselves, while the other two classes lend their force in drawing the minds of perceivers to it as an object as a magnet draws a piece of iron. Their functionings at this time are undoubtedly feeble (*sūkshmavṛttimantaḥ*) but still they do exist. *

In the three guṇas, none of them can be held as the goal

* See Bhikshu's *Yoga-vārttika*, II. 18.

of the others. All of them are equally important, and the very varied nature of the manifold represents only the different combinations of these guṇas as substantive entities. In any combination one of the guṇas may be more predominant than the others, but the other guṇas are also present there and perform their functions in their own way. No one of them is more important than the other, but they serve conjointly one common purpose, viz. the experiences and the liberation of the purusha, or spirit. They are always uniting, separating and re-uniting again and there is neither beginning nor end of this (*anyonyamithunāḥ sarvve naishāmādisamprayogo viprayogo vā upalabhyate*).

They have no purpose of their own to serve, but they all are always evolving, as Dr. Seal says, " ever from a relatively less differentiated, less determinate, less coherent whole, to a relatively more differentiated, more determinate, more coherent whole " * for the experiences and liberation of purusha, or spirit. When in a state of equilibrium they cannot serve the purpose of the purusha, so that state of the guṇas is not for the sake of the purusha ; it is its own independent eternal state. All the other three stages of evolution, viz. the liṅga (sign), aviśesha (unspecialised) and viśesha (specialised) have been caused for the sake of the purusha.† Thus Vyāsa writes:— ‡ " The objects of the purusha are no cause of the original state (*aliṅga*). That is to say, the fulfilment of the objects of the purusha is not the cause which brings about the manifestation of the original state of prakṛti in the beginning. The fulfilment of the objects of the purusha is not therefore the reason of the existence of that ultimate state. Since it is not brought into existence by the need of the fulfilment of the purusha's objects it is said to be eternal. As to the three

* *History of Hindu Chemistry*, Vol. II, by P. C. Ray, p. 66.

† The usual Sāṃkhya terms as found in Īśvarakṛshṇa's *Kārikā*, having the same denotation as aviśesha and viśesha, are *prakṛtivikṛti* and *vikṛti*.

‡ *Vyāsa-bhāshya*, II. 19.

specialised states, the fulfilment of the objects of the purusha becomes the cause of their manifestation in the beginning. The fulfilment of the objects of the purusha is not therefore the reason for the existence of the cause. Since it is not brought into existence by the purusha's objects it is said to be eternal. As to the three specialised states, the fulfilment of the objects of the purusha being the cause of their manifestation in the beginning, they are said to be non-eternal."

Vācaspati again says:—"The fulfilment of the objects of the purusha could be said to be the cause of the original state, if that state could bring about the fulfilment of the objects of the purusha, such as the enjoyment of sound, etc., or manifest the discrimination of the distinction between true self and other phenomena. If however it did that, it could not be a state of equilibrium," (*yadyaliṅgāvasthā śabdādyupabhogam vā sattvapurushānyatākhyātim vā purushārtham nirvarttayet tannrvarttane hi na sāmyāvasthā syāt*). This state is called the prakṛti. It is the beginning, indeterminate, unmediated and undetermined. It neither exists nor does it not exist, but is the principium of almost all existence. Thus Vyāsa describes it as "the state which neither is nor is not; that which exists and yet does not; that in which there is no non-existence; the unmanifested, the noumenon (lit. without any manifested indication), the background of all" (*niḥsattāsattam niḥsadasat nirasat avyaktam aliṅgam pradhānam*).* Vācaspati explains it as follows:—"Existence consists in possessing the capacity of effecting the fulfilment of the objects of the purusha. Non-existence means a mere imaginary trifle (e.g. the horn of a hare)." It is described as being beyond both these states of existence and non-existence. The state of the equipoise of the three guṇas of intelligence-stuff, inertia and energy, is nowhere of use in fulfilling the objects of the purusha. It

* *Vyāsa-bhāshya*, II. 19.

therefore does not exist as such. On the other hand, it does not admit of being rejected as non-existent like an imaginary lotus of the sky. It is therefore not non-existent. But even allowing the force of the above arguments about the want of phenomenal existence of prakṛti on the ground that it cannot serve the objects of the purusha, the difficulty arises that the principles of Mahat, etc., exist in the state of the unmanifested also, because nothing that exists can be destroyed; and if it is destroyed, it cannot be born again, because nothing that does not exist can be born ; it follows therefore that since the principles of mahat, etc., exist in the state of the unmanifested, that state can also affect the fulfilment of the objects of the purusha. How then can it be said that the unmanifested is not possessed of existence ? For this reason, he describes it as that in which it exists and does not exist. This means that the cause exists in that state in a potential form but not in the form of the effect. Although the effect exists in the cause as mere potential power, yet it is incapable of performing the function of fulfilling the objects of the purusha ; it is therefore said to be non-existent as such. Further he says that this cause is not such, that its effect is of the nature of hare's horn. It is beyond the state of non-existence, that is, of the existence of the effect as mere nothing. If it were like that, then it would be like the lotus of the sky and no effect would follow.*

But as Bhikshu points out (*Yoga-vārttika*, II. 18) this prakṛti is not simple substance, for it is but the guṇa reals. It is simple only in the sense that no complex qualities are manifested in it. It is the name of the totality of the guṇa reals existing in a state of equilibrium through their mutual counter opposition. It is a hypothetical state of the guṇas preceding the states in which they work in mutual co-operation for the creation of the cosmos for giving the purushas

* *Tattvavaiśāradī*, II. 19.

a chance for ultimate release attained through a full enjoyment of experiences. Some European scholars have often asked me whether the prakṛti were real or whether the guṇas were real. This question, in my opinion, can only arise as a result of confusion and misapprehension, for it is the guṇas in a state of equilibrium that are called prakṛti. Apart from guṇas there is no prakṛti (*guṇā eva prakṛtiśabdavācyā na tu tadatiriktā prakṛtirasti. Yoga-vārttika*, II. 18). In this state, the different guṇas only annul themselves and no change takes place, though it must be acknowledged that the state of equipoise is also one of tension and action, which, however, being perfectly balanced does not produce any change. This is what is meant by evolution of similars (*adṛśapariṇāma*). Prakṛti as the equilibrium of the three guṇas is the absolute ground of all the mental and phenomenal modifications—pure potentiality.

Veṅkaṭa, a later Vaishṇava writer, describes prakṛti as one ubiquitous, homogeneous matter which evolves itself into all material productions by condensation and rarefaction. In this view the guṇas would have to be translated as three different classes of qualities or characters, which are found in the evolutionary products of the prakṛti. This will of course be an altogether different view of the prakṛti from that which is described in the *Vyāsa-bhāshya*, and the guṇas could not be considered as reals or as substantive entities in such an interpretation. A question arises, then, as to which of these two prakṛtis is the earlier conception. I confess that it is difficult to answer it. For though the Vaishṇava view is elaborated in later times, it can by no means be asserted that it had not quite as early a beginning as 2nd or 3rd century B.C. If *Ahirbudhnyasamhitā* is to be trusted then the *Shashṭitantra-śāstra* which is regarded as an authoritative Sāṃkhya work is really a Vaishṇava work. Nothing can be definitely stated about the nature of prakṛti in Sāṃkhya from the meagre statement of the *Kārikā*. The statement in the *Vyāsa-bhāshya* is, however, definitely in favour of the interpretation that we have adopted, and so also the *Sāṃkhya-sūtra*, which is most probably a later work. Caraka's account of prakṛti does not seem to be the prakṛti of *Vyāsa-bhāshya* for here the guṇas are not regarded as reals or substantive entities, but as characters, and prakṛti is regarded as containing its evolutes, mahat, etc., as its elements (*dhātu*). If Caraka's treatment is the earliest view of Sāṃkhya that is available to us, then it has to be admitted that the earliest Sāṃkhya view did not accept prakṛti as a state of the guṇas, or guṇas as substantive entities. But the *Yoga-sūtra*, II. 19, and the *Vyāsa-bhāshya* support the interpretation that I have adopted here, and it is very curious that if the Sāṃkhya view was known at the time to be so different from it, no reference to it should have been made. But whatever may be the original Sāṃkhya view, both the Yoga view and the later Sāṃkhya view are quite in consonance with my interpretation.

In later Indian thinkers there had been a tendency to make a compromise between the Vedānta and Sāṃkhya doctrines and to identify prakṛti with the avidyā of the Vedāntists. Thus Lokācāryya writes :—"It is called prakṛti since it is the source of all change, it is called avidyā since it is opposed to knowledge, it is called māyā since it is the cause of diversion creation (*prakṛtirityucyate vikārotpādakatvāt avidyā jñāna-virodhitvāt māyā vicitrasṛshṭikaratvāt*)."* But this is distinctly opposed to the *Vyāsa-bhāshya* which defines avidyā as *vidyāviparītaṃ jñānāntaraṃ avidyā*, i.e. avidyā is that other knowledge which is opposed to right knowledge. In some of the Upanishads, *Svetāśvatara* for example, we find that māyā and prakṛti are identified and the great god is said to preside over them (*māyāṃ tu prakṛtiṃ vidyāt māyinaṃ tumaheśvaraṃ*). There is a description also in the Ṛgveda, X. 92, where it is

* *Tattvatraya*, p. 48 (Chowkhamba edition), Benares.

said that (*nāsadāsīt na sadāsīt tadānīṃ*), in the beginning there was neither the " Is " nor the " Is not," which reminds one of the description of prakṛti (*niḥsattāsattaṃ* as that in which there is no existence or non-existence). In this way it may be shown from *Gītā* and other Sanskrit texts that an undifferentiated, unindividuated cosmic matter as the first principle, was often thought of and discussed from the earliest times. Later on this idea was utilised with modifications by the different schools of Vedāntists, the Sāmkhyists and those who sought to make a reconciliation between them under the different names of prakṛti, avidyā and māyā. What avidyā really means according to the Pātañjala system we shall see later on; but here we see that whatever it might mean it does not mean prakṛti according to the Pātañjala system. *Vyāsa-bhāshya*, IV. 13, makes mention of māyā also in a couplet from *Shashṭitantraśāstra*;

guṇānāṃ paramaṃ rūpaṃ na dṛshṭipathamṛcchati
yattu dṛshṭipathaṃ prāptaṃ tanmāyeva sutucch akaṃ.

The real appearance of the guṇas does not come within the line of our vision. That, however, which comes within the line of vision is but paltry delusion and Vācaspati Miśra explains it as follows :—Prakṛti is like the māyā but it is not māyā. It is trifling (*sutucchaka*) in the sense that it is changing. Just as māyā constantly changes, so the transformations of prakṛti are every moment appearing and vanishing and thus suffering momentary changes. Prakṛti being eternal is real and thus different from māyā.

This explanation of Vācaspati's makes it clear that the word māyā is used here only in the sense of illusion, and without reference to the celebrated māyā of the Vedāntists; and Vācaspati clearly says that prakṛti can in no sense be called māyā, since it is real.*

* Bhikshu in his *Yoga-vārttika* explains " *māyeva* " as " *laukikamāyeva kshaṇabhaṅguram* " evanescent like the illusions of worldly experience.

CHAPTER II

PURUSHA

We shall get a more definite notion of prakṛti as we advance further into the details of the later transformations of the prakṛti in connection with the purushas. The most difficult point is to understand the nature of its connection with the purushas. Prakṛti is a material, non-intelligent, independent principle, and the souls or spirits are isolated, neutral, intelligent and inactive. Then how can the one come into connection with the other ?

In most systems of philosophy the same trouble has arisen and has caused the same difficulty in comprehending it rightly. Plato fights the difficulty of solving the unification of the idea and the non-being and offers his participation theory ; even in Aristotle's attempt to avoid the difficulty by his theory of form and matter, we are not fully satisfied, though he has shown much ingenuity and subtlety of thought in devising the " expedient in the single conception of development."

The universe is but a gradation between the two extremes of potentiality and actuality, matter and form. But all students of Aristotle know that it is very difficult to understand the true relation between form and matter, and the particular nature of their interaction with each other, and this has created a great divergence of opinion among his commentators. It was probably to avoid this difficulty that the dualistic appearance of the philosophy of Descartes had to be reconstructed in the pantheism of Spinoza. Again we find also how Kant failed to bring about the relation between noumenon and phenomenon, and created two worlds absolutely unrelated to each other. He tried to reconcile the schism that he effected in his *Critique of Pure Reason* by his *Critique of Practical Reason*, and again supplemented it with his *Critique of Judgment*, but met only with dubious success.

In India also this question has always been a little puzzling, and before trying to explain the Yoga point of view, I shall first give some of the other expedients devised for the purpose, by the different schools of Advaita (monistic) Vedāntism.

I. The reflection theory of the Vedānta holds that the māyā is without beginning, unspeakable, mother of gross matter, which comes in connection with intelligence, so that by its reflection in the former we have Īśvara. The illustrations that are given to explain it both in *Siddhāntaleśa** and in *Advaita-Brahmasiddhi* are only cases of physical reflection, viz. the reflection of the sun in water, or of the sky in water.

II. The limitation theory of the Vedānta holds that the all-pervading intelligence must necessarily be limited by mind, etc., so of necessity it follows that " the soul " is its limitation. This theory is illustrated by giving those common examples in which the Ākāśa (space) though unbounded in itself is often spoken of as belonging to a jug or limited by the jug and as such appears to fit itself to the shape and form of the jug and is thus called *ghaṭāvacchinna ākāśa*, i.e. space as within the jug.

Then we have a third school of Vedāntists, which seeks to explain it in another way:—The soul is neither a reflection nor a limitation, but just as the son of Kuntī was known as the son of Rādhā, so the pure Brahman by his nescience is known as the jīva, and like the prince who was brought up in the family of a low caste, it is the pure Brahman who by his own

* *Siddhāntalleśa* (Jīveśvara nirūpaṇa).

nescience undergoes birth and death, and by his own nescience is again released.*

The *Sāṃkhya-sūtra* also avails itself of the same story in IV. 1, "*rājaputtravattattvopadeśāt,*" which Vijñāna Bhikshu explains as follows :—A certain king's son in consequence of his being born under the star Gaṇḍa having been expelled from his city and reared by a certain forester remains under the idea : "I am a forester." Having learnt that he is alive, a certain minister informs him. "Thou art not a forester, thou art a king's son." As he, immediately having abandoned the idea of being an outcast, betakes himself to his true royal state, saying, "I am a king," so too the soul realises its purity in consequence of instruction by some good tutor, to the effect —"Thou, who didst originate from the first soul, which manifests itself merely as pure thought, art a portion thereof."

In another place there are two sūtras :—(1) *niḥsaṅge'pi uparāgo vivekāt.* (2) *japāsphaṭikayoriva noparāgaḥ kintvabhimānaḥ.* (1) Though it be associated still there is a tingeing through non-discrimination. (2) As in the case of the hibiscus and the crystal, there is not a tinge, but a fancy. Now it will be seen that all these theories only show that the transcendent nature of the union of the principle of pure intelligence is very difficult to comprehend. Neither the reflection nor the limitation theory can clear the situation from vagueness and incomprehensibility, which is rather increased by their physical illustrations, for the cit or pure intelligence cannot undergo reflection like a physical thing, nor can it be obstructed or limited by it. The reflection theory adduced by the *Sāṃkhya-sūtra,* "*japāsphiṭikayoriva noparāgaḥ kintvabhimānaḥ,*"

* Princess Kuntī of the Mahābhārata had a son born to her by means of a charm when she was still a virgin. Being afraid of a public scandal she floated the child in a stream ; the child was picked up by the wife of a carpenter (Rādhā). The boy grew up to be the great hero Karṇa and he thought that he was the son of a carpenter until the fact of his royal lineage was disclosed to him later in life.

is not an adequate explanation. For here the reflection produces only a seeming redness of the colourless crystal, which was not what was meant by the Vedāntists of the reflection school. But here, though the metaphor is more suitable to express the relation of purusha with the prakṛti, the exact nature of the relation is more lost sight of than comprehended. Let us now see how Patañjali and Vyāsa seek to explain it.

Let me quote a few sūtras of Patañjali and some of the most important extracts from the *Bhāshya* and try, as far as possible, to get the correct view :—

(1) *dṛgdarśanaśaktyorekātmateva asmitā* II. 6.

(2) *drashṭā dṛśiṃātraḥ śuddho'pi pratyayānupaśyaḥ* II. 20.

(3) *tadartha eva dṛśyasya ātmā* II. 21.

(4) *kṛtārthaṃ prati nashṭamapyanashṭaṃ tadanyasādhāraṇatvāt* II. 22.

(5) *Svasvāmiśaktyoḥ svarūpopalabdhihetuḥ saṃyogaḥ* II. 22.

(6) *tadabhāvāt saṃyogābhāvo hānaṃ taddṛśeḥ kaivalyaṃ* II. 25.

(7) *sattvapurushayoḥ śuddhisāmye kaivalyaṃ* III. 25.

(8) *citerapratisaṃkramāyāstadākārāpattau svabuddhisaṃvedanaṃ* IV. 22.

(9) *sattvapurushayoratyantāsaṅkīrṇayoḥ pratyayāviśesho bhogaḥ parārthatvāt svārthasaṃyamāt purushajñānam* III. 35.

(1) The Ego-sense is the illusory appearance of the identity of the power as perceiver and the power as perceived.

(2) The seer though pure as mere "seeing" yet perceives the forms assumed by the psychosis (*buddhi*).

(3) It is for the sake of the purusha that the being of the knowable exists.

(4) For the emancipated person the world-phenomena cease to exist, yet they are not annihilated since they form a common field of experience for other individuals.

(5) The cause of the realisation of the natures of the knowable and purusha in consciousness is their mutual contact.

(6) Cessation is the want of mutual contact arising from the destruction of ignorance and this is called the state of oneness.

(7) This state of oneness arises out of the equality in purity of the purusha and buddhi or sattva.

(8) Personal consciousness arises when the purusha, though in its nature unchangeable, is cast into the mould of the psychosis.

(9) Since the mind-objects exist only for the purusha, experience consists in the non-differentiation of these two which in their natures are absolutely distinct; the knowledge of self arises out of concentration on its nature.

Thus in *Yoga-sūtra*, II. 6, dṛik or purusha the seer is spoken of as śakti or power as much as the prakṛti itself, and we see that their identity is only apparent. Vyāsa in his *Bhāshya* explains *ekātmatā* (unity of nature or identity) as *avibhāga-prāptāviva*, "as if there is no difference." And Pañcaśikha, as quoted in *Vyāsa-bhāshya*, writes: "not knowing the purusha beyond the mind to be different therefrom, in nature, character and knowledge, etc., a man has the notion of self, in the mind through delusion."

Thus we see that when the mind and purusha are known to be separated, the real nature of purusha is realised. This seeming identity is again described as that which perceives the particular form of the mind and thereby appears, as identical with it though it is not so (*pratyayānupaśya—pratyayāni bauddhamanupaśyati tamanupaśyannatadātmāpi tadātmaka iva pratibhāti*, *Vāysa-bhāshya*, II. 20).

The purusha thus we see, cognises the phenomena of consciousness after they have been formed, and though its nature is different from conscious states yet it appears to be the same. Vyāsa in explaining this sūtra says that purusha is neither quite similar to the mind nor altogether different from it.

For the mind (*buddhi*) is always changeful, according to the change of the objects that are offered to it; so that it may be said to be changeful according as it knows or does not know objects; but the purusha is not such, for it always appears as the self, being reflected through the mind by which it is thus connected with the phenomenal form of knowledge. The notion of self that appears connected with all our mental phenomena and which always illumines them is only due to this reflection of purusha in the mind. All phenomenal knowledge which has the form of the object can only be transformed into conscious knowledge as "I know this," when it becomes connected with the self or purusha. So the purusha may in a way be said to see again what was perceived by the mind and thus to impart consciousness by transferring its illumination into the mind. The mind suffers changes according to the form of the object of cognition, and thus results a state of conscious cognition in the shape of "I know it," when the mind, having assumed the shape of an object, becomes connected with the constant factor purusha, through the transcendent reflection or identification of purusha in the mind. This is what is meant by *pratyayānupaśya* reperception of the mind-transformations by purusha, whereby the mind which has assumed the shape of any object of consciousness becomes intelligent. Even when the mind is without any objective form, it is always being seen by purusha. The exact nature of this reflection is indeed very hard to comprehend; no physical illustrations can really serve to make it clear. And we see that neither the *Vyāsa-bhāshya* nor the sūtras offer any such illustrations as Sāṃkhya did. But the *Bhāshya* proceeds to show the points in which the mind may be said to differ from purusha, as well as those in which it agrees with it. So that though we cannot express it anyhow, we may at least make some advance towards conceiving the situation.

Thus the *Bhāshya* says that the main difference between the mind and purusha is that the mind is constantly undergoing modifications, as it grasps its objects one by one; for the grasping of an object, the act of having a percept, is nothing but its own undergoing of different modifications, and thus, since an object sometimes comes within the grasp of the mind and again disappears in the subconscious as a saṃskāra (potency) and again comes into the field of the understanding as smṛti (memory), we see that it is pariṇāmi or changing. But purusha is the constant seer of the mind when it has an object, as in ordinary forms of phenomenal knowledge, or when it has no object as in the state of nirodha or cessation. Purusha is unchanging. It is the light which remains unchanged amidst all the changing modifications of the mind, so that we cannot distinguish purusha separately from the mind. This is what is meant by saying *buddheḥ pratisaṃvedī purushaḥ*, i.e. purusha reflects or turns into its own light the concepts of mind and thus is said to know it. Its knowing is manifested in our consciousness as the ever-persistent notion of the self, which is always a constant factor in all the phenomena of consciousness. Thus purusha always appears in our consciousness as the knowing agent. Truly speaking, however, purusha only sees himself; he is not in any way in touch with the mind. He is absolutely free from all bondage, absolutely unconnected with prakṛti. From the side of appearance he seems only to be the intelligent seer imparting consciousness to our conscious-like conception, though in reality he remains the seer of himself all the while. The difference between purusha and prakṛti will be clear when we see that purusha is altogether independent, existing in and for himself, free from any bondage whatsoever; but buddhi exists on the other hand for the enjoyment and release of purusha. That which exists in and for itself, must ever be the self-same, unchangeable entity, suffering no transformations or modifications, for it has no other end owing to which it will be liable to change. It is the self-centred, self-satisfied light, which never seeks any other end and never leaves itself. But prakṛti is not such ; it is always undergoing endless, complex modifications and as such does not exist for itself but for purusha, and is dependent upon him. The mind is unconscious, while purusha is the pure light of intelligence, for the three guṇas are all non-intelligent, and the mind is nothing but a modification of these three guṇas which are all non-intelligent.

But looked at from another point of view, prakṛti is not altogether different from purusha ; for had it been so how could purusha, which is absolutely pure, reperceive the mind-modifications ? Thus the *Bhāshya* (II. 20) writes :—

" Well then let him be dissimilar. To meet this he says : He is not quite dissimilar. Why ? Although pure, he sees the ideas after they have come into the mind. Inasmuch as purusha cognises the ideas in the form of mind-modification, he appears to be, by the act of cognition, the very self of the mind although in reality he is not." As has been said, the power of the enjoyer, purusha (*dṛkśakti*), is certainly unchangeable and it does not run after every object. In connection with a changeful object it appears forever as if it were being transferred to every object and as if it were assimilating its modifications. And when the modifications of the mind assume the form of the consciousness by which it is coloured, they imitate it and look as if they were manifestations of purusha's consciousness unqualified by the modifications of the non-intelligent mind.

All our states of consciousness are analysed into two parts —a permanent and a changing part. The changing part is the form of our consciousness, which is constantly varying according to the constant change of its contents. The permanent part is that pure light of intelligence, by virtue of which we have the notion of self reflected in our consciousness. Now, as this self persists through all the varying changes of the objects of consciousness, it is inferred that the light which thus shines in our consciousness is unchangeable. Our mind is constantly suffering a thousand modifications, but the notion of self is the only thing permanent amidst all this change. It is this self that imports consciousness to the material parts of our knowledge. All our concepts originated from our perception of external material objects. Therefore the forms of our concepts which could exactly and clearly represent these material objects in their own terms, must be made of a stuff which in essence is not different from them. But with the reflection of purusha, the soul, the notion of self comes within the content of our consciousness, spiritualising, as it were, all our concepts and making them conscious and intelligent. Thus this seeming identity of purusha and the mind, by which purusha may be spoken of as the seer of the concept, appears to the self, which is manifested in consciousness by virtue of the seeming reflection. For this is that self, or personality, which remains unchanged all through our consciousness. Thus our phenomenal intelligent self is partially a material reality arising out of the seeming interaction of the spirit and the mind. This interaction is the only way by which matter releases spirit from its seeming bondage.

But the question arises, how is it that there can even be a seeming reflection of purusha in the mind which is altogether non-intelligent? How is it possible for the mind to catch a glimpse of purusha, which illuminates all the concepts of consciousness, the expression "*anupaśya*" meaning that he perceives by imitation (*anukāreṇa paśyati*)? How can purusha, which is altogether formless, allow any reflection of itself to imitate the form of buddhi, by virtue of which it appears as the self—the supreme possessor and knower of all our mental conceptions ? There must be at least some resemblance between the mind and the purusha, to justify in some sense this seeming reflection. And we find that the last sūtra of the Vibhūtipāda says : *sattvapurushayoḥ śuddhisāmye kaivalyaṃ*—which means that when the sattva or the preponderating mind-stuff becomes as pure as purusha, kaivalya or oneness is attained. This shows that the pure nature of sattva has a great resemblance to the pure nature of purusha. So much so, that the last stage preceding the state of kaivalya, is almost the same as kaivalya itself, when purusha is in himself and there are no thoughts to reflect. In this state, we see that the mind can be so pure as to reflect exactly the nature of purusha, as he is in himself. This state in which the mind becomes as pure as purusha and reflects him in his purity, does not materially differ from the state of kaivalya, in which purusha is in himself—the only difference being that the mind, when it becomes so pure as this, becomes gradually lost in prakṛti and cannot again serve to bind purusha.

I cannot refrain here from the temptation of referring to a beautiful illustration from Vyāsa, to explain the way in which the mind serves the purposes of purusha. *Cittamayaskāntamaṇikalpaṃ sannidhimātropakāri dṛśyatvena svaṃ bhavati purushasya svāminaḥ* (I. 4), which is explained in *Yoga-vārttika* as follows : *Tathāyaskāntamaṇiḥ svasminneva ayaḥsannidhīkaraṇamātrāt śalyarishkarshaṇākhyam upakāram kurvat purushasya svāminaḥ svam bhavati bhogasādhanatvāt*, i.e. just as a magnet draws iron towards it, though it remains unmoved itself, so the mind-modifications become drawn towards purusha, and thereby become visible to purusha and serve his purpose.

To summarise : We have seen that something like a union takes place between the mind and purusha, i.e. there is a seeming reflection of purusha in the mind, simultaneously with its being determined conceptually, as a result whereof this reflection of purusha in the mind, which is known as the self, becomes united with these conceptual determinations of the mind and the former is said to be the perceiver of all these determinations. Our conscious personality or self is thus the seeming unity of the knowable as the mind in the shape of conceptual or judgmental representations with the reflections of purusha in the mind. Thus, in the single act of cognition, we have the notion of our own personality and the particular conceptual or perceptual representation with which this ego identifies itself. The true seer, the pure intelligence, the free, the eternal, remains all the while beyond any touch of impurity from the mind, though it must be remembered that it is its own seeming reflection in the mind that appears as the ego, the cogniser of all our states, pleasures and sorrows of the mind and one who is the apperceiver of this unity of the seeming reflection—of purusha and the determinations of the mind. In all our conscious states, there is such a synthetic unity between the determinations of our mind and the self, that they cannot be distinguished one from the other—a fact which is exemplified in all our cognitions, which are the union of the knower and the known. The nature of this reflection is a transcendent one and can never be explained by any physical illustration. Purusha is altogether different from the mind, inasmuch as he is the pure intelligence and is absolutely free, while the latter is non-intelligent and dependent on purusha's enjoyment and release, which are the sole causes of its movement. But there is some similarity between the two, for how could the mind otherwise catch a seeming glimpse of him? It is also said that the pure mind can adapt itself to the pure form of purusha; this is followed by the state of kaivalya.

We have discussed the nature of purusha and its general relations with the mind. We must now give a few more illustrations. The chief point in which purusha of the Sāṃkhya-Pātañjala differs from the similar spiritual principle of Vedānta is, that it regards its soul, not as one, but as many. Let us try to discuss this point, in connection with the arguments of the Sāṃkhya-Pātañjala doctrine in favour of a separate principle of purusha. Thus the *Kārikā* says: *saṃghātaparārthatvāt triguṇādiviparyyayādadhishthānāt purusho'sti bhoktṛbhāvāt kaivalyārthaṃ pravṛtteśca,** "Because an assemblage of things is for the sake of another; because there must be an entity different from the three guṇas and the rest (their modifications); because there must be a superintending power; because there must be someone who enjoys; and because of (the existence of) active exertion for the sake of abstraction or isolation (from the contact with prakṛti) therefore the soul exists." The first argument is from design or teleology by which it is inferred that there must be some other simple entity for which these complex collocations of things are intended. Thus Gauḍapāda says: "In such manner as a bed, which is an assemblage of bedding, props, cotton, coverlet and pillows, is for another's use, not for its own, and its several component parts render no mutual service, and it is concluded that there is a man who sleeps upon the bed and for whose sake it was made; so this world, which is an assemblage of the five elements, is for use and there is a soul, for whose enjoyment this body, another's consisting of intellect and the rest, has been produced."†

The *second argument* is that all the knowable is composed of just three elements: first, the element of sattva, or intelligence-stuff, causing all manifestations; second, the element of rajas or energy, which is ever causing transformations; and third, tamas, or the mass, which enables rajas to actualise. Now such a prakṛti, composed of these three elements, cannot itself be a seer. For the seer must be always

* *Kārikā* 17. † Gauḍapāda's commentary on *Kārikā* 17.

the same unchangeable, actionless entity, the ever present, ever constant factor in all stages of our consciousness.

Third argument: There must be a supreme background of pure consciousness, all our co-ordinated basis of experience. This background is the pure actionless purusha, reflected in which all our mental states become conscious. Davies explains this a little differently, in accordance with a simile in the *Tattva-Kaumudī, yathā rathādi yantrādibhiḥ,* thus: "This idea of Kapila seems to be that the power of self-control cannot be predicted of matter, which must be directed or controlled for the accomplishment of any purpose, and this controlling power must be something external to matter and diverse from it. The soul, however, never acts. It only seems to act; and it is difficult to reconcile this part of the system with that which gives to the soul a controlling force. If the soul is a charioteer, it must be an active force." But Davies here commits the mistake of carrying the simile too far. The comparison of the charioteer and the chariot holds good, to the extent that the chariot can take a particular course only when there is a particular purpose for the charioteer to perform. The motion of the chariot is fulfilled only when it is connected with the living person of the charioteer, whose purpose it must fulfil.

Fourth argument: Since prakṛti is non-intelligent, there must be one who enjoys its pains and pleasures. The emotional and conceptual determinations of such feelings are aroused in consciousness by the seeming reflection of the light of purusha.

Fifth argument: There is a tendency in all persons to move towards the oneness of purusha, to be achieved by liberation; there must be one for whose sake the modifications of buddhi are gradually withheld, and a reverse process set up, by which they return to their original cause prakṛti and thus liberate purusha. It is on account of this reverse tendency of prakṛti to release purusha that a man feels prompted to achieve his liberation as the highest consummation of his moral ideal.

Thus having proved the existence of purusha, the *Kārikā* proceeds to prove his plurality: "*janmamaraṇakaraṇānāṃ pratiniyamādayugapat pravṛtteśca purushabahutvaṃ siddhaṃ traiguṇyaviparyyayācca.*" "From the individual allotment of birth, death and the organs; from diversity of occupations and from the different conditions of the three guṇas, it is proved that there is a plurality of souls." In other words, since with the birth of one individual, all are not born; since with the death of one, all do not die; and since each individual has separate sense organs for himself; and since all beings do not work at the same time in the same manner; and since the qualities of the different guṇas are possessed differently by different individuals, purushas are many. Patañjali, though he does not infer the plurality of purushas in this way, yet holds the view of the sūtra, *kṛtārthaṃ prati nashṭamapyanashṭaṃ tadanyasādhāraṇatvāt.* "Although destroyed in relation to him whose objects have been achieved, it is not destroyed, being common to others."

Davies, in explaining the former *Kārikā*, says: "There is, however, the difficulty that the soul is not affected by the three guṇas. How can their various modifications prove the individuality of souls in opposition to the Vedāntist doctrine, that all souls are only portions of the one, an infinitely extended monad?"

This question is the most puzzling in the Sāṃkhya doctrine. But careful penetration of the principles of Sāṃkhya-Yoga would make clear to us that this is a necessary and consistent outcome of the Sāṃkhya view of a dualistic universe.

For if it is said that purusha is one and we have the notion of different selves by his reflection into different minds, it follows that such notions as self, or personality, are false. For the only true being is the one, purusha. So the knower being false, the known also becomes false; the knower and the known having vanished, everything is reduced to that which we can in no way conceive. It may be argued that according to the Sāṃkhya philosophy also, the knower is false, for the pure purusha as such is not in any way connected with prakṛti. But even then it must be observed that the Sāṃkhya-Yoga view does not hold that the knower is false but analyses the nature of the ego and says that it is due to the seeming unity of the mind and purusha, both of which are reals in the strictest sense of the term. Purusha is there justly called the knower. He sees and simultaneously with this, there is a modification of buddhi (mind); this seeing becomes joined with this modification of buddhi and thus arises the ego, who perceives that particular form of the modification of buddhi. Purusha always remains the knower. Buddhi suffers modifications and at the same time catches a glimpse of the light of purusha, so that contact (*saṃyoga*) of purusha and prakṛti occurs at one and the same point of time, in which there is unity of the reflection of purusha and the particular transformation of buddhi.

The knower, the ego and the knowable, are none of them false in the Sāṃkhya-Yoga system at the stage preceding kaivalya, when buddhi becomes as pure as purusha; its modification resembles the exact form of purusha and then purusha knows himself in his true nature in buddhi; after which buddhi vanishes. The Vedānta has to admit the modifications of māyā, but must at the same time hold it to be unreal. The Vedānta says that māyā is as beginningless as prakṛti yet has an ending with reference to the released person as the buddhi of the Sāṃkhyists.

But according to the Vedānta philosophy, knowledge of ego is only false knowledge—an illusion as many imposed upon the formless Brahman. Māyā, according to the Vedāntist, can neither be said to exist nor to non-exist. It is *anirvācyā*, i.e. can never be described or defined. Such an unknown and unknowable māyā causes the Many of the world by reflection upon the Brahman. But according to the Sāṃkhya doctrine, prakṛti is as real as purusha himself. Prakṛti and purusha are two irreducible metaphysical remainders whose connection is beginningless (*anādisaṃyoga*). But this connection is not unreal in the Vedānta sense of the term. We see that according to the Vedānta system, all notions of ego or personality are false and are originated by the illusive action of the māyā, so that when they ultimately vanish there are no other remainders. But this is not the case with Sāṃkhya, for as purusha is the real seer, his cognitions cannot be dismissed as unreal, and so purushas or knowers as they appear to us to be, must be held real. As prakṛti is not the māyā of the Vedāntist (the nature of whose influence over the spiritual principle cannot be determined) we cannot account for the plurality of purushas by supposing that one purusha is being reflected into many minds and generating the many egos. For in that case it will be difficult to explain the plurality of their appearances in the minds (buddhis). For if there be one spiritual principle, how should we account for the supposed plurality of the buddhis ? For we should rather expect to find one buddhi and not many to serve the supposed one purusha, and this will only mean that there can be only one ego, his enjoyment and release. Supposing for argument's sake that there are many buddhis and one purusha, which reflected in them, is the cause of the plurality of selves, then we cannot see how prakṛti is moving for the enjoyment and release of one purusha; it would rather appear to be moved for the sake of the enjoyment and release of the reflected or unreal self. For purusha is not finally released with the release of any number of particular individual selves. For it may be released with reference to one individual but remain bound to others. So prakṛti would not really be moved in this hypothetical case for the sake of purusha, but for the sake of the reflected selves only. If we wish to avoid the said difficulties, then with the release of one purusha, all purushas will have to be released. For in the supposed theory there would not really be many different purushas, but the one purusha appearing as many, so that with his release all the other so-called purushas must be released. We see that if it is the enjoyment (*bhoga*) and salvation (*apavarga*) of one purusha which appear as so many different series of enjoyments and emancipations, then with his experiences all should have the same experiences. With his birth and death, all should be born or all should die at once. For, indeed, it is the experiences of one purusha which appear in all the seeming different purushas. And in the other suppositions there is neither emancipation nor enjoyment by purusha at all. For there, it is only the illusory self that enjoys or releases himself. By his release no purusha is really released at all. So the fundamental conception of prakṛti as moving for the sake of the enjoyment and release of purusha has to be abandoned.

So we see that from the position in which Sāṃkhya and Yoga stood, this plurality of the purushas was the most consistent thing that they could think of. Any compromise with the Vedānta doctrine here would have greatly changed the philosophical aspect and value of the Sāṃkhya philosophy. As the purushas are nothing but pure intelligences they can as well be all pervading though many. But there is another objection that, since number is a conception of the phenomenal mind, how then can it be applied to the purushas which are said to be many ?* But that difficulty remains unaltered

* Purusha is a substance (*dravya*) because it has independent existence (*anāśrita*) and has a measure (*vibhu parimāṇa*) of its own. So it always possesses the common characteristics (*sāmānya guṇa*) of substances, contact (*saṃyoga*), separation (*viyoga*) and number (*saṃkhyā*). Purusha cannot be considered to be suffering change or impure on account of the possession of the above common characteristics of all substances. *Yoga-vārttika*, II. 17.

even if we regard the purusha as one. When we go into the domain of metaphysics and try to represent Reality with the symbols of our phenomenal conceptions we have really to commit almost a violence towards it. But we must perforce do this in all our attempts to express in our own terms that pure, inexpressible, free illumination which exists in and for itself beyond the range of any mediation by the concepts or images of our mind. So we see that Sāṃkhya was not inconsistent in holding the doctrine of the plurality of the purushas. Patañjali does not say anything about it, since he is more anxious to discuss other things connected with the presupposition of the plurality of purusha. Thus he speaks of it only in one place as quoted above and says that though for a released person this world disappears altogether, still it remains unchanged in respect to all the other purushas.

CHAPTER III

THE REALITY OF THE EXTERNAL WORLD

WE may now come to the attempt of Yoga to prove the reality of an external world as against the idealistic Buddhists. In sūtra 12 of the chapter on kaivalya we find: "The past and the future exist in reality, since all qualities of things manifest themselves in these three different ways. The future is the manifestation which is to be. The past is the appearance which has been experienced. The present is that which is in active operation. It is this threefold substance which is the object of knowledge. If it did not exist in reality, there would not exist a knowledge thereof. How could there be knowledge in the absence of anything knowable? For this reason the past and present in reality exist."*

So we see that the present holding within itself the past and the future exists in reality. For the past though it has been negated has really been preserved and kept in the present, and the future also though it has not made its appearance yet exists potentially in the present. So, as we know the past and the future worlds in the present, they both exist and subsist in the present. That which once existed cannot die, and that which never existed cannot come to be (*nāstyasataḥ saṃbhavaḥ na cāsti sato vināsāḥ*, *Vyāsa-bhāshya* V. 12). So the past has not been destroyed but has rather shifted its

* Thus the *Bhāshya* says: *bhavishyadvyaktikamanāgataṃanudbhūtavyaktikamatītaṃ svavyāpāropārūḍhaṃ varttamānaṃ trayaṃ caitadvastu jñānasya jñeyam yadi caitat svarūpato nābhavishyannedaṃ nirvishayaṃ jñānamudapatsyata tasmādatītamanāgataṃ svarūpato'stīti.*

position and hidden itself in the body of the present, and the future that has not made its appearance exists in the present only in a potential form. It cannot be argued, as Vācaspati says, that because the past and the future are not present therefore they do not exist, for if the past and future do not exist how can there be a present also, since its existence also is only relative ? So all the three exist as truly as any one of them, and the only difference among them is the different way or mode of their existence.

He next proceeds to refute the arguments of those idealists who hold that since the external knowables never exist independently of our knowledge of them, their separate external existence as such may be denied. Since it is by knowledge alone that the external knowables can present themselves to us we may infer that there is really no knowable external reality apart from knowledge of it, just as we see that in dream-states knowledge can exist apart from the reality of any external world.

So it may be argued that there is, indeed, no external reality as it appears to us. The Buddhists, for example, hold that a blue thing and knowledge of it as blue are identical owing to the maxim that things which are invariably perceived together are one (*sahopalambhaniyamādabhedo nīlataddhiyoḥ*). So they say that external reality is not different from our idea of it. To this it may be replied that if, as you say, external reality is identical with my ideas and there is no other external reality existing as such outside my ideas, why then does it appear as existing apart, outside and independent of my ideas ? The idealists have no basis for the denial of external reality, and for their assertion that it is only the creation of our imagination like experiences in dreams. Even our ideas carry with them the notion that reality exists outside our mental experiences. If all our percepts and notions as this and that arise only by virtue of the influence of the external world, how can they deny the existence of the external world as such ? The objective world is present by its own power. How then can this objective world be given up on the strength of mere logical or speculative abstraction ?

Thus the *Vyāsa-bhāshya*, IV. 14, says : "There is no object without the knowledge of it, but there is knowledge as imagined in dreams without any corresponding object; thus the reality of external things is like that of dream-objects, mere imagination of the subject and unreal. How can they who say so be believed ? Since they first suppose that the things which present themselves to us by their own force do so only on account of the invalid and delusive imagination of the intellect, and then deny the reality of the external world on the strength of such an imaginary supposition of their own."

The external world has generated knowledge of itself by its own presentative power (*arthena svakīyayāgrāhyaśaktyā vijñānamajani*), and has thus caused itself to be represented in our ideas, and we have no right to deny it.* Commenting on the *Bhāshya* IV. 14, Vācaspati says that the method of agreement applied by the Buddhists by their *sahopalambhaniyama* (maxim of simultaneous revelation) may possibly be confuted by an application of the method of difference. The method of agreement applied by the idealists when put in proper form reads thus : "Wherever there is knowledge there is external reality, or rather every case of knowledge agrees with or is the same as every case of the presence of external reality, so knowledge is the cause of the presence of the external reality, i.e. the external world depends for its reality on our knowledge or ideas and owes its origin or appearance as such to them." But Vācaspati says that this application of the method of agreement is not certain, for it cannot be corroborated by the method of difference. For

* *Tattravaiśāradī*, IV. 14.

the statement that every case of absence of knowledge is also a case of absence of external reality cannot be proved, i.e. we cannot prove that the external reality does not exist when we have no knowledge of it (*sahopalambhaniyamaśca vedyatvañca hetū sandigdhavyatirekatayānaikāntikau*) IV. 14.

Describing the nature of grossness and externality, the attributes of the external world, he says that grossness means the pervading of more portions of space than one, i.e. grossness means extension, and externality means being related to separate space, i.e. co-existence in space. Thus we see that extension and co-existence in space are the two fundamental qualities of the gross external world. Now an idea can never be said to possess them, for it cannot be said that an idea has extended into more spaces than one and yet co-existed separately in separate places. An idea cannot be said to exist with other ideas in space and to extend in many points of space at one and the same time. To avoid this it cannot be said that there may be plurality of ideas so that some may co-exist and others may extend in space. For co-existence and extension can never be asserted of our ideas, since they are very fine and subtle, and can be known only at the time of their individual operation, at which time, however, other ideas may be quite latent and unknown. Imagination has no power to negate their reality, for the sphere of imagination is quite distinct from the sphere of external reality, and it can never be applied to an external reality to negate it. Imagination is a mental function, and as such has no touch with the reality outside, which it can by no means negate.

Further it cannot be said that, because grossness and externality can abide neither in the external world nor in our ideas, they are therefore false. For this falsity cannot be thought as separable from our ideas, for in that case our ideas would be as false as the false itself. The notion of externality and grossness pervades all our ideas, and if they are held to be false, no true thing can be known by our ideas and they therefore become equally false.

Again, knowledge and the external world can never be said to be identical because they happen to be presented together. For the method of agreement cannot by itself prove identity. Knowledge and the knowable external world may be independently co-existing things like the notions of existence and non-existence. Both co-exist independently of one another. It is therefore clear enough, says Vācaspati, that the certainty arrived at by perception, which gives us a direct knowledge of things, can never be rejected on the strength of mere logical abstraction or hair-splitting discussion.

We further see, says Patañjali, that the thing remains the same though the ideas and feelings of different men may change differently about it.* Thus A, B, C may perceive the same identical woman and may feel pleasure, pain or hatred. We see that the same common thing generates different feelings and ideas in different persons; external reality cannot be said to owe its origin to the idea or imagination of any one man, but exists independently of any person's imagination in and for itself. For if it be due to the imagination of any particular man, it is his own idea which as such cannot generate the same ideas in another man. So it must be said that the external reality is what we perceive it outside.

There are, again, others who say that just as pleasure and pain arise along with our ideas and must be said to be due to them so the objective world also must be said to have come into existence along with our ideas. The objective world therefore according to these philosophers has no external existence either in the past or in the future, but has only a momentary existence in the present due to our ideas about it. That much existence only are they ready to attribute to external objects which can be measured by the idea of the

* *Vastusāmye cittabhedāt tayor vibhaktaḥ panthāḥ.* *Yoga-sūtra*, IV. 15.

moment. The moment I have an idea of a thing, the thing rises into existence and may be said to exist only for that moment and as soon as the idea disappears the object also vanishes, for when it cannot be presented to me in the form of ideas it can be said to exist in no sense. But this argument cannot hold good, for if the objective reality should really depend upon the idea of any individual man, then the objective reality corresponding to an idea of his ought to cease to exist either with the change of his idea, or when he directs attention to some other thing, or when he restrains his mind from all objects of thought. Now, then, if it thus ceases to exist, how can it again spring into existence when the attention of the individual is again directed towards it? Again, all parts of an object can never be seen all at once. Thus supposing that the front side of a thing is visible, then the back side which cannot be seen at the time must not be said to exist at all. So if the back side does not exist, the front side also can as well be said not to exist (*ye cāsyānupasthitā bhāgaste cāsya na syurevaṃ nāsti pṛshṭhamiti udaramapi na gṛhyeta. Vyāsa-bhāshya*, IV. 16). Therefore it must be said that there is an independent external reality which is the common field of observation for all souls in general; and there are also separate "Cittas" for separate individual souls (*tasmāt svatantro'rthaḥ sarvapurushasādhāraṇaḥ svatantrāṇi ca cittāni pratipurushaṃ, pravarttante, ibid.*). And all the experiences of the purusha result from the connection of this "Citta" (mind) with the external world.

Now from this view of the reality of the external world we are confronted with another question—what is the ground which underlies the manifold appearance of this external world which has been proved to be real? What is that something which is thought as the vehicle of such qualities as produce in us the ideas? What is that self-subsistent substratum which is the basis of so many changes, actions and reactions that we always meet in the external world? Locke called this substratum substance and regarded it as unknown, but said that though it did not follow that it was a product of our own subjective thought yet it did not at the same time exist without us. Hume, however, tried to explain everything from the standpoint of association of ideas and denied all notions of substantiality. We know that Kant, who was much influenced by Hume, agreed to the existence of some such unknown reality which he called the Thing-in-itself, the nature of which, however, was absolutely unknowable, but whose influence was a great factor in all our experiences.

But the *Bhāshya* tries to penetrate deeper into the nature of this substratum or substance and says: *dharmisvarūpamātro hi dharmaḥ, dharmivikriyā eva eshā dharmadvārā prapañcyate*, *Vyāsa-bhāshya*, III. 13. The characteristic qualities form the very being itself of the characterised, and it is the change of the characterised alone that is detailed by means of the characteristic. To understand thoroughly the exact significance of this statement it will be necessary to take a more detailed review of what has already been said about the guṇas. We know that all things mental or physical are formed by the different collocations of sattva of the nature of illumination (*prakāśa*), rajas—the energy or mutative principle of the nature of action (*kriyā*)—and tamas—the obstructive principle of the nature of inertia (*sthiti*) which in their original and primordial state are too fine to be apprehended (*gunānāṃparamaṃ rūpaṃ na dṛshṭipathamṛcchati*, *Vyāsa-bhāshya*, IV. 13). These different guṇas combine in various proportions to form the manifold universe of the knowable, and thus are made the objects of our cognition. Through combining in different proportions they become, in the words of Dr. B. N. Seal, "more and more differentiated, determinate and coherent," and thus make themselves cognisable, yet they never forsake their own true nature as the guṇas. So we see that they have thus got two natures, one in which they remain quite unchanged as guṇas, and another in which they collocate and combine themselves in various ways and thus appear under the veil of a multitude of qualities and states of the manifold knowable (*te vyaktasūkshmā guṇātmānaḥ* [IV. 13] . . . *sarvamidaṃ guṇānāṃ sanniveśaviśeshamātramiti paramārthato guṇātmānaḥ, Bhāshya, ibid.*).

Now these guṇas take three different courses of development from the ego or ahaṃkāra according to which the ego or ahaṃkāra may be said to be sāttvika, rājasa and tāmasa. Thus from the sāttvika side of the ego by a preponderance of sattva the five knowledge-giving senses, e.g. hearing, sight, touch, taste and smell are derived. From the rajas side of ego by a preponderance of rajas the five active senses of speech, etc., are derived. From the tamas side of ego or ahaṃkāra by a preponderance of tamas are derived the five tanmātras. From which again by a preponderance of tamas the atoms of the five gross elements—earth, water, fire, air and ether are derived.

In the derivation of these it must be remembered that all the three guṇas are conjointly responsible. In the derivation of a particular product one of the guṇas may indeed be predominant, and thus may bestow the prominent characteristic of that product, but the other two guṇas are also present there and perform their functions equally well. Their opposition does not withhold the progress of evolution but rather helps it. All the three combine together in varying degrees of mutual preponderance and thus together help the process of evolution to produce a single product. Thus we see that though the guṇas are three, they combine to produce on the side of perception, the senses, such as those of hearing, sight, etc.; and on the side of the knowable, the individual tanmātras of gandha, rasa, rūpa, sparśa and śabda. The guṇas composing each tanmātra again harmoniously combine with each other with a preponderance of tamas to produce the atoms of each gross element. Thus in each combination one class of guṇas remains prominent, while the others remain dependent upon it but help it indirectly in the evolution of that particular product.

CHAPTER IV

THE PROCESS OF EVOLUTION

THE evolution which we have spoken of above may be characterised in two ways: (1) That arising from modifications or products of some other cause which are themselves capable of originating other products like themselves; (2) That arising from causes which, though themselves derived, yet cannot themselves be the cause of the origination of other existences like themselves. The former may be said to be slightly specialised (*aviśesha*) and the latter thoroughly specialised (*viśesha*).

Thus we see that from prakṛti comes mahat, from mahat comes ahaṃkāra, and from ahaṃkāra, as we have seen above, the evolution takes three different courses according to the preponderance of sattva, rajas and tamas originating the cognitive and conative senses and manas, the superintendent of them both on one side and the tanmātras on the other. These tanmātras again produce the five gross elements. Now when ahaṃkāra produces the tanmātras or the senses, or when the tanmātras produce the five gross elements, or when ahaṃkāra itself is produced from buddhi or mahat, it is called *tattvāntara-pariṇāma*, i.e. the production of a different tattva or substance.

Thus in the case of *tattvāntara-pariṇāma* (as for example when the tanmātras are produced from ahaṃkāra), it must be carefully noticed that the state of being involved in the tanmātras is altogether different from the state of being of ahaṃkāra ; it is not a mere change of quality but a change of existence or state of being.* Thus though the tanmātras are derived from ahaṃkāra the traces of ahaṃkāra cannot be easily followed in them. This derivation is not such that the ahaṃkāra remains principally unchanged and there is only a change of quality in it, but it is a different existence altogether, having properties which differ widely from those of ahaṃkāra. So it is called tattvāntara-pariṇāma, i.e. evolution of different categories of existence.

Now the evolution that the senses and the five gross elements can undergo can never be of this nature, for they are viśeshas, or substances which have been too much specialised to allow the evolution of any other substance of a different grade of existence from themselves. With them there is an end of all emanation. So we see that the aviśeshas or slightly specialised emanations are those which being themselves but emanations can yet yield other emanations from themselves. Thus we see that mahat, ahaṃkāra and the five tanmātras are themselves emanations, as well as the source of other emanations. Mahat, however, though it is undoubtedly an aviśesha or slightly specialised emanation, is called by another technical name liṅga or sign, for from the state of mahat, the prakṛti from which it must have emanated may be inferred. Prakṛti, however, from which no other primal state is inferable, is called the aliṅga or that which is not a sign for the existence of any other primal and more unspecialised state. In one sense all the emanations can be with justice called the liṅgas or states of existence standing as the sign by which the causes from

* "*Tattvāntara-pariṇāma*" means the evolution of a wholly new category of existence. Thus the tanmātras are wholly different from the ego from which they are produced. So the atoms are wholly different from the tanmātras from which they are produced, for the latter, unlike the former, have no sense-properties. In all combinations of atoms, there would arise thousands of new qualities, but none of the products of the combination of atoms can be called a tattvāntara, or a new category of existence since all these qualities are the direct manifestations of the specific properties of the atoms.

which they have emanated can be directly inferred. Thus in this sense the five gross elements may be called the liṅga of the tanmātras, and they again of the ego, and that again of the mahat, for the unspecialised ones are inferred from their specialised modifications or emanations. But this technical name liṅga is reserved for the mahat from which the aliṅga or prakṛti can be inferred. This prakṛti, however, is the eternal state which is not an emanation itself but the basis and source of all other emanations.

The liṅga and the aliṅga have thus been compared in the *Kārikā*:

"*hetumadanityamavyāpi sakriyamanekāśritaṃ liṅgaṃ*
sāvayavam paratantraṃ vyaktaṃ viparītamavyaktaṃ."

The liṅga has a cause, it is neither eternal nor universal, but mobile, multiform, dependent, determinate, and possesses parts, whereas the aliṅga is the reverse. The aliṅga or prakṛti, however, being the cause has some characteristics in common with its liṅgas as distinguished from the purushas, which are altogether different from it.

Thus the *Kārikā* says:

"*triguṇamaviveki vishayaḥ sāmānyamacetanaṃ prasavadharmi*
vyaktaṃ tathā pradhānaṃ tadviparītastathā pumān."

The manifested and the unmanifested *pradhāna* or *prakṛti* are both composed of the three guṇas, non-intelligent, objective, universal, unconscious and productive. Soul in these respects is the reverse. We have seen above that prakṛti is the state of equilibrium of the guṇas, which can in no way be of any use to the purushas, and is thus held to be eternal, though all other states are held to be non-eternal as they are produced for the sake of the purushas.

The state of prakṛti is that in which the guṇas completely overpower each other and the characteristics (*dharma*) and the characterised (*dharmī*) are one and the same.

Evolution is thus nothing but the manifestation of change, mutation, by the energy of rajas. The rajas is the one mediating activity that breaks up all compounds, builds up new ones and initiates original modifications. Whenever in any particular combination the proportion of sattva, rajas or tamas alters, as a condition of this alteration, there is the dominating activity of rajas by which the old equilibrium is destroyed and another equilibrium established; this in its turn is again disturbed and again another equilibrium is restored. Now the manifestation of this latent activity of rajas is what is called change or evolution. In the external world the time that is taken by a paramāṇu or atom to move from its place is identical with a unit of change.* Now an atom will be that quantum which is smaller or finer than that point or limit at which it can in any way be perceived by the senses. Atoms are therefore mere points without magnitude or dimension, and the unit of time or moment (*kshaṇa*) that is taken up in changing the position of these

* *Vyāsa-bhāshya*, III. 52, says that the smallest indivisible part of a thing is called a paramāṇu. Vijñāna Bhikshu in explaining it says that paramāṇu here means guṇa, for if a thing say a stone is divided, then the furthest limit of division is reached when we come to the indivisible guṇas. But if the prakṛti is all-pervading (*vibhu*) how can the guṇas be atomic? Bhikshu says (*Yoga-vārttika*, III. 52) in reply that there are some classes of guṇas (e.g. those which produce mind *antaḥkaraṇa* and *ākāśa*) which are all-pervading, while the others are all atomic. In Bhikshu's interpretation a moment is to be defined as the time which a guṇa entity takes to change its own unit of space. Guṇas are thus equivalent to the Vaiśeshika paramāṇus. Bhikshu, however, does not deny that there are no atoms of earth, water, etc., but he says that where reference is not made to these atoms but to guṇa atoms for the partless units of time can only be compared with the partless guṇas. But Vācaspati does not make any comment here to indicate that the smallest indivisible unit of matter should mean guṇas. Moreover, *Yoga-sūtra*, I. 40, and *Vyāsa-bhāshya*, I. 45, speak of *paramāṇu* and *aṇu* in the sense of earth-atoms, etc. Even Bhikshu does not maintain that paramāṇu is used there in the sense of atomic guṇa entities. I could not therefore accept Bhikshu's interpretation that paramāṇu here refers to guṇa. Paramāṇu may here be taken in the sense of material atoms of earth, water, etc. The atoms (paramāṇu) here cannot be absolutely partless, for it has two sides, prior (*pūrvadeśa*) and posterior (*uttaradeśa*).

atoms is identical with one unit of change or evolution. The change or evolution in the external world must therefore be measured by these units of spatial motion of the atoms; i.e. an atom changing its own unit of space is the measure of all physical change or evolution.

Each unit of time (*kshaṇa*) corresponding to this change of an atom of its own unit of space is the unit-measure of change. This instantaneous succession of time as discrete moments one following the other is the notion of the series of moments or pure and simple succession. Now the notion of these discrete moments is the notion of time. Even the notion of succession is one that does not really exist but is imagined, for a moment comes into being just when the moment just before had passed so that they have never taken place together. Thus Vyāsa in III. 52, says: "*kshaṇatatkramayornāsti vastusamāhāraḥ iti buddhisamāhāraḥ muhūrttāhorātrātrādayaḥ.*" *Sa tvayaṃ kālaḥ vastuśūnyo'pi buddhinirmāṇaḥ.* The moments and their succession do not belong to the category of actual things; the hour, the day and night, are all aggregates of mental conceptions. This time which is not a substantive reality in itself, but is only a mental concept, represented to us through linguistic usage, appears to ordinary minds as if it were an objective reality.

So the conception of time as discrete moments is the real one, whereas the conception of time as successive or as continuous is unreal, being only due to the imagination of our empirical and relative consciousness. Thus Vācaspati further explains it. A moment is real (*vastupatitaḥ*) and is the essential element of the notion of succession. Succession involves the notion of change of moments, and the moment is called time by those sages who know what time is. Two moments cannot happen together. There cannot be any succession of two simultaneous things. Succession means the notion of change involving a preceding and a succeeding moment. Thus there is only the present moment and there are no preceding and later moments. Therefore there cannot be any union of these moments. The past and the future moments may be said to exist only if we speak of past and future as identical with the changes that have become latent and others that exist potentially but are not manifested. Thus in one moment, the whole world suffers changes. All these characteristics are associated with the thing as connected with one particular moment.*

So we find here that time is essentially discrete, being only the moments of our cognitive life. As two moments never co-exist, there is no succession or continuous time. They exist therefore only in our empirical consciousness which cannot take the real moments in their discrete nature but connects the one with the other and thereby imagines either succession or continuous time.

Now we have said before, that each unit of change or evolution is measured by this unit of time *kshaṇa* or moment; or rather the units of change are expressed in terms of these moments or *kshaṇas*. Of course in our ordinary consciousness these moments of change cannot be grasped, but they can be reasonably inferred. For at the end of a certain period we observe a change in a thing; now this change, though it becomes appreciable to us after a long while, was still going on every moment, so, in this way, the succession of evolution or change cannot be distinguished from the moments coming one after another. Thus the *Yoga-sūtra* says in IV. 33: "Succession involving a course of changes is associated with the moments." Succession as change of moments is grasped

* Bhikshu regards the movement of a guṇa of its own unit of space as the ultimate unit of time (*kshaṇa*). The whole world is nothing else but a series of *kshaṇas*. This view differs from the Buddhist view that everything is momentary in this that it does not admit of any other thing but the *kshaṇas* (*na tu kshaṇātiriktaḥ kshaṇikaḥ padārthaḥ kaścidishyate taistu kshaṇamātrasthāyyeva padārthaḥ ishyate*. *Yoga-vārttika*, III. 52).

only by a course of changes. A cloth which has not passed through a course of changes through a series of moments cannot be found old all at once at any time. Even a new cloth kept with good care becomes old after a time. This is what is called the termination of a course of changes and by it the succession of a course of changes can be grasped. Even before a thing is old there can be inferred a sequence of the subtlest, subtler, subtle, grossest, grosser and gross changes (*Tattvavaiśāradī*, IV. 33).*

Now as we have seen that the unit of time is indistinguishable from the unit of change or evolution, and as these moments are not co-existing but one follows the other, we see that there is no past or future existing as a continuous before or past, and after or future. It is the present that really exists as the manifested moment; the past has been conserved as sublatent and the future as the latent. So the past and future exist in the present, the former as one which has already had its manifestation and is thus conserved in the fact of the manifestation of the present. For the manifestation of the present as such could not have taken place until the past had already been manifested; so the manifestation of the present is a concrete product involving within itself the manifestation of the past; in a similar way it may be said that the manifestation of the present contains within itself the seed or the unmanifested state of the future, for if this had not been the case, the future never could have happened. So we see that the whole world undergoes a change at one unit

* There is a difference of opinion as regards the meaning of the word "*kshaṇapratiyogi*" in IV. 33. Vācaspati says that it means the growth associated with a particular *kshaṇa* or moment (*kshaṇapracayāśraya*). The word *pratiyogī* is interpreted by Vācaspati as related (*pratisambandhī*). Bhikshu, however, gives a quite different meaning. He interprets *kshaṇa* as "interval" and pratiyogī as "opposite of" (*virodhī*). So "*kshaṇapratiyogī*" means with him "without any interval" or "continuous." He holds that the sūtra means that all change is continuous and not in succession. There is according to his interpretation no interval between the cessation of a previous character and the rise of a new one.

point of time, and not only that but it conserves within itself all the past and future history of cosmic evolution.

We have pointed out before that the manifestation of the rajas or energy as action is what is called change. Now this manifestation of action can only take place when equilibrium of a particular collocation of guṇas is disturbed and the rajas arranges or collocates with itself the sattva and tamas, the whole group being made intelligible by the inherent sattva. So the cosmic history is only the history of the different collocations of the guṇas. Now, therefore, if it is possible for a seer to see in one vision the possible number of combinations that the rajas will have with sattva and tamas, he can in one moment perceive the past, present or future of this cosmic evolutionary process; for with such minds all past and future are concentrated at one point of vision which to a person of ordinary empirical consciousness appears only in the series. For the empirical consciousness, impure as it is, it is impossible that all the powers and potencies of sattva and rajas should become manifested at one point of time; it has to take things only through its senses and can thus take the changes only as the senses are affected by them; whereas, on the other hand, if its power of knowing was not restricted to the limited scope of the senses, it could have grasped all the possible collocations or changes all at once. Such a perceiving mind whose power of knowing is not narrowed by the senses can perceive all the finest modifications or changes that are going on in the body of a substance (see *Yoga-sūtra*, III. 53).

CHAPTER V

THE EVOLUTION OF THE CATEGORIES

THE Yoga analysis points to the fact that all our cognitive states are distinguished from their objects by the fact of their being intelligent. This intelligence is the constant factor which persists amidst all changes of our cognitive states. We are passing continually from one state to another without any rest, but in this varying change of these states we are never divested of intelligence. This fact of intelligence is therefore neither the particular possession of any one of these states nor that of the sum of these states ; for if it is not the possession of any one of these states it cannot be the possession of the sum of these states. In the case of the released person again there is no mental state, but the self-shining intelligence. So Yoga regarded this intelligence as quite distinct from the so-called mental states which became intelligent by coming in connection with this intelligence. The actionless, absolutely pure and simple intelligence it called the purusha.

Yoga tacitly assumed a certain kind of analysis of the nature of these mental states which sought to find out, if possible, the nature of their constituent elements or moments of existence. Now in analysing the different states of our mind we find that a particular content of thought is illuminated and then passed over. The ideas rise, are illuminated and pass away. Thus they found that "movement" was one of the principal elements that constituted the substance of our thoughts. Thought as such is always moving. This principle of movement, mutation or change, this energy, they called rajas.

Now apart from this rajas, thought when seen as divested of its sensuous contents seems to exhibit one universal mould or form of knowledge which assumes the form of all the sensuous contents that are presented to it. It is the one universal of all our particular concepts or ideas—the basis or substratum of all the different shapes imposed upon itself, the pure and simple. Sattva in which there is no particularity is that element of our thought which, resembling purusha most, can attain its reflection within itself and thus makes the unconscious mental states intelligible. All the contents of our thought are but modes and limitations of this universal form and are thus made intelligible. It is the one principle of intelligibility of all our conscious states.

Now our intellectual life consists in a series of shining ideas or concepts ; concepts after concepts shine forth in the light of the pure intelligence and pass away. But each concept is but a limitation of the pure shining universal of our knowledge which underlies all its changing modes or modifications of concepts or judgments. This is what is called pure knowledge in which there is neither the knower nor the known. This pure object—subjectless knowledge differs from the pure intelligence or purusha only in this that later on it is liable to suffer various modifications, as the ego, the senses, and the infinite percepts and concepts, etc., connected therewith, whereas the pure intelligence remains ever pure and changeless and is never the substratum of any change. At this stage sattva, the intelligence-stuff, is prominent and rajas and tamas are altogether suppressed. It is for this reason that the buddhi or mind is often spoken of as the sattva. Being an absolute preponderance of sattva it has nothing else to manifest, but it is its pure shining self.

Both tamas and rajas being mostly suppressed they cannot in any way affect the effulgent nature of this pure shining of contentless knowledge in which there is neither the knower nor the known.

But it must be remembered that it is holding suspended as it were within itself the elements of rajas and tamas which cannot manifest themselves owing to the preponderance of the sattva.

This notion of pure contentless consciousness is immediate and abstract and as such is at once mediated by other necessary phases. Thus we see that this pure contentless universal consciousness is the same as the ego-universal (*asmitāmātra*). For this contentless universal consciousness is only another name for the contentless unlimited, infinite of the ego-universal. A quotation from Fichte may here be useful as a comparison. Thus he says in the introduction to his *Science of Ethics:* "How an object can ever become a subject, or how a being can ever become an object of representation: this curious change will never be explained by anyone who does not find a point where the objective and subjective are not distinguished at all, but are altogether one. Now such a point is established by, and made the starting point of our system. This point is the Egohood, the Intelligence, Reason, or whatever it may be named."* The *Vyāsa-bhāshya*, II. 19, describes it as *liṅgamātram mahattatvaṃ sattāmātre mahati ātmani*, and again in I. 36 we find it described as the waveless ocean, peaceful infinite pure egohood. This obscure egohood is known merely as being. This mahat has also been spoken of by Vijñāna Bhikshu as the manas, or mind, as it has the function of assimilation (*niścaya*). Now what we have already said about mahat will, we hope, make it

* Nothing more than a superficial comparison with Fichte is here intended. A large majority of the texts and the commentary literature would oppose the attempts of all those who would like to interpret Sāṃkhya-yoga on Fichtean lines.

clear that this mahat is the last limit at which the subject and the object can be considered as one indistinguishable point which is neither the one nor the other, but the source of both.

This buddhi is thus variously called *mahat*, *asmitāmātra*, *manas*, *sattva*, *buddhi* and *liṅga*, according to the aspects from which this state is observed.

This state is called mahat as it is the most universal thing conceivable and the one common source from which all other things originate.

Now this phase of sattva or pure shining naturally passes into the other phase, that of the Ego as knower or Ego as subject. The first phase as mahat or asmitāmātra was the state in which the sattva was predominant and the rajas and tamas were in a suppressed condition. The next moment is that in which the rajas comes uppermost, and thus the ego as the subject of all cognition—the subject I—the knower of all the mental states—is derived. The contentless subject-objectless "I" is the passive sattva aspect of the buddhi catching the reflection of the spirit of purusha.

In its active aspect, however, it feels itself one with the spirit and appears as the ego or subject which knows, feels and wills. Thus Patañjali says, in II. 6: *dṛgdarśanaśaktyorekātmateva asmitā*, i.e. the seeming identity of the seer and the perceiving capacity is called asmitā-ego. Again in *Bhāshya*, I. 17, we have *ekātmikā saṃvidasmitā* (knowledge as one identical is asmitā) which Vācaspati explains as *sā ca ātmanā grahītrā saha buddhirekātmikā saṃvid*, i.e. it is the feeling of identity of the buddhi (mind) with the self, the perceiver. Thus we find that the mind is affected by its own rajas or activity and posits itself as the ego or subject as activity. By reason of this position of the "I" as active it perceives itself in the objective, in all its conative and cognitive senses in its thoughts and feelings and also in the external world of extension and co-existence; in the words of Pañcaśikha (II. 5) thinking the animate and inanimate beings to be the self, man regards their prosperity as his own and becomes glad, and regards their adversity as his own and is sorry. Here the "I" is posited as the active entity which becomes conscious of itself, or in other words the "I" becomes self-conscious. In analysing this notion of self-consciousness we find that here the rajas or element of activity or mobility has become predominant and this predominance of rajas has been manifested by the inherent sattva. Thus we find that the rajas side or "I as active" has become manifested or known as such, i.e. "I" becomes conscious of itself as active. And this is just what is meant by self-consciousness.

This ego or self-consciousness then appears as the modification of the contentless pure consciousness of the mind (*buddhi*); it is for this reason that we see that this self-consciousness is but a modification of the universal mind. The absolute identity of subject and object as the egohood is not a part of our natural consciousness, for in all stages of our actual consciousness, even in that of self-consciousness, there is an element of the preponderance of rajas or activity which directs this unity as the knower and the known and then unites them as it were. Only so far as I distinguish myself as the conscious, from myself as the object of consciousness, am I at all conscious of myself.

When we see that the buddhi transforms itself into the ego, the subject, or the knower, at this its first phase there is no other content which it can know, it therefore knows itself in a very abstract way as the "I," or in other words, the ego becomes self-conscious; but at this moment the ego has no content; the tamas being quite under suppression, it is evolved by a preponderance of the rajas; and thus its nature as rajas is manifested by the sattva and thus the ego now essentially knows itself to be active, and holds itself as the permanent energising activity which connects with itself all the phenomena of our life.

But now when the ego first directs itself towards itself and becomes conscious of itself, one question which naturally comes to our mind is, "Can the ego direct itself towards itself and thus divide itself into a part that sees and one that is seen?" To meet this question it is assumed that the guṇas contain within themselves the germs of both subjectivity and objectivity (*guṇānāṃ hi dvairūpyaṃ vyavasāyātmkatvam vyavaseyātmakatvaṃ ca. Tattvavaiśāradī*, III. 47); the guṇas have two forms, the perceiver and the perceived. Thus we find that in the ego the quality of the guṇas as the perceiver comes to be first manifested and the ego turns back upon itself and makes itself its own object. It is at this stage that we are reminded of the twofold nature of the guṇas.

It is by virtue of this twofold nature that the subject can make itself its own object; but as these two sides have not yet developed they are still only abstract and exist but in an implicit way in this state of the ego (*ahaṃkāra*).

Enquiring further into the nature of the relation of this ego and the buddhi, we find that the ego is only another phase or modification of the buddhi; however different it might appear from buddhi it is only an appearance or phase of it; its reality is the reality of the buddhi. Thus we see that when the knower is affected in his different modes of concepts and judgments, this too is to be ascribed to the buddhi. Thus Vyāsa writes (II. 18) that perception, memory, differentiation, reasoning, right knowledge, decision belong properly to mind (buddhi) and are only illusorily imposed on the purusha (*grahaṇadhāraṇohāpohatattvajñānābhiniveśā buddhau vartamānā purushe adhyāropitasadbhāvāḥ*).

Now from this ego we find that three developments take place in three distinct directions according to the preponderance of sattva, rajas or tamas.

By the preponderance of rajas, the ego develops itself into the five conative senses, vāk (speech), pāṇi (hands), pāda (feet), pāyu (organ of passing the excreta) and upastha (generative organ). By the preponderance of sattva, the ego develops itself into the five cognitive senses—hearing, touch, sight, taste and smell; and by a preponderance of tamas it stands as the bhūtādi and produces the five tanmātras, and these again by further preponderance of tamas develops into the particles of the five gross elements of earth, water, light, heat, air and ether.

Now it is clear that when the self becomes conscious of itself as object we see that there are three phases in it: (i) that in which the self becomes an object to itself; (ii) when it directs itself or turns as the subject upon itself as the object, this moment of activity which can effect an aspect of change in itself; (iii) the aspect of the consciousness of the self, the moment in which it perceives itself in its object, the moment of the union of itself as the subject and itself as the object in one luminosity of self-consciousness. Now that phase of self in which it is merely an object to itself is the phase of its union with prakṛti which further develops the prakṛti in moments of materiality by a preponderance of the inert tamas of the bhūtādi into tanmātras and these again into the five grosser elements which are then called the *grāhya* or perceptible.

The sattva side of this ego or self-consciousness which was hitherto undifferentiated becomes further differentiated, specialised and modified into the five cognitive senses with their respective functions of hearing, touch, sight, taste and smell, synchronising with the evolution of the prakṛti on the tanmātric side of evolution. These again individually suffer infinite modifications themselves and thus cause an infinite variety of sensations in their respective spheres in our conscious life. The rajas side of the ego becomes specialised as the active faculties of the five different conative organs.

There is another specialisation of the ego as the manas which is its direct instrument for connecting itself with the five cognitive and conative senses. What is perceived as mere sensations by the senses is connected and generalised and formed into concepts by the manas; it is therefore spoken of as partaking of both the conative and the cognitive aspects in the *Sāṃkhya-kārikā*, 27.

Now though the modifications of the ego are formed successively by the preponderance of sattva, rajas and tamas, yet the rajas is always the accessory cause (*sahakāri*) of all these varied collocations of the guṇas; it is the supreme principle of energy and supplies even intelligence with the energy which it requires for its own conscious activity. Thus Lokācāryya says in his *Tattvatraya*: "the tāmasa ego developing into the material world and the sāttvika ego developing into the eleven senses, both require the help of the rājasa ego for the production of this development" (*anyābhyāṃ ahaṃkārābhyām svakāryyopajanane rājasāhaṃkāraḥ sahakārī bhavati*); and Barabara in his *Bhāshya* writes: "just as a seed-sprout requires for its growth the help of water as instrumental cause, so the rājasa ahaṃkāra (ego) works as the accessory cause (*sahakāri*) for the transformations of sāttvika and tāmasa ahaṃkāra into their evolutionary products." The mode of working of this instrumental cause is described as "rajas is the mover." The rājasa ego thus moves the sattva part to generate the senses; the tamas part generating the gross and subtle matter is also moved by the rajas, agent of movement. The rājasa ego is thus called the common cause of the movement of the sāttvika and the tāmasa ego. Vācaspati also says: "though rajas has no separate work by itself yet since sattva and tamas (which though capable of undergoing modification, do not do their work) are actionless in themselves, the agency of rajas lies in this that it moves them both for the production of the effect."* And according as the modifications are sāttvika, tāmasa or rājasika, the ego which is the cause of these different modifications is also called vaikārika, bhūtādi and taijasa. The mahat also as the source of the vaikārika, taijasa and bhūtādi ego may be said to have three aspects.

Now speaking of the relation of the sense faculties with the sense organs, we see that the latter, which are made up of the grosser elements are the vehicle of the former, for if the latter are injured in any way, the former are also necessarily affected.†

To take for example the specific case of the faculty of hearing and its organ, we see that the faculty of hearing is seated in the ether (*ākāśa*) within our ear-hole. It is here that the power of hearing is located. When soundness or defect is noticed therein, soundness or defect is noticed in the power of hearing also. When the sounds of solids, etc., are heard, then the power of hearing located in the hollow of the ear stands in need of the resonance produced in the ākāśa of the ear.

This sense of hearing, then, having its origin in the principle of ahaṃkāra, behaves like iron, and is drawn by the sounds originated and located in the mouth of the speaker acting as loadstone, and transforms them into its own successive modifications (*vṛtti*) and thus senses the sounds of the speaker. And it is for this reason that for every living creature, the perception of sound in external space in the absence of ḍefects is never void of authority, Thus Pancasikha also says, as quoted in *Vyāsa-bhāshya*, III. 41:

* *Tattvakaumudī* on *Sāṃkhya-kārikā*, 25.
† *Tattvavaiśāradī*, III. 41.

"To all those whose organs of hearing are situated in the same place (at different times) the ākāśa sustaining the sense of hearing is the same." The ākāśa, again, in which the power of hearing is seated, is born out of the soniferous tanmātra, and has therefore the quality of sound inherent in itself. It is by this sound acting in unison that it takes the sounds of external solids, etc. This then proves that the ākāśa is the substratum of the power of hearing, and also possesses the quality of sound. And this sameness of the situation of sound is an indication of the existence of ākāśa as that which is the substratum of the auditory power (*śruti*) which manifests the sounds of the same class in ākāśa. Such a manifestation of sound cannot be without such an auditory sense-power. Nor is such an auditory power a quality of pṛthivī (earth), etc., because it cannot be in its own self both the manifestor and the manifested (*vyaṅgya* and *vyañjaka*), *Tattvavaiśāradī*, III. 41. It is the auditory power which manifests all sounds with the help of the ākāśa of the sense organ.

The theory of the guṇas was accepted by many others outside the Sāmkhya-Yoga circle and they also offered their opinions on the nature of the categories.

There are thus other views prevalent about the genesis of the senses, to which it may be worth our while to pay some attention as we pass by.

The sāttvika ego in generating the cognitive senses with limited powers for certain specified objects of sense only accounted for their developments from itself in accompaniment with the specific tanmātras. Thus

sāttvika ego+sound potential (śabda-tanmātra)=sense of hearing.

sāttvika ego+touch potential (śparś-tanmātra)=sense of touch.

sāttvika ego+sight potential (śrūpa-tanmātra)=sense of vision.

sāttvika ego+taste potential (vasa-tanmātra)=sense of taste.

sāttvika ego+smell potential (gandha-tanmātra)=sense of smell.

The conative sense of speech is developed in association with the sense of hearing; that of hand in association with the sense of touch; that of feet in association with the sense of vision; that of upastha in association with the sense of taste; that of pāyu in association with the sense of smell.

Last of all, the manas is developed from the ego without any co-operating or accompanying cause.

The Naiyāyikas, however, think that the senses are generated by the gross elements, the ear for example by ākāśa, the touch by air and so forth. But Lokācāryya in his *Tattvatraya* holds that the senses are not generated by gross matter but are rather sustained and strengthened by it.

There are others who think that the ego is the instrumental and that the gross elements are the material causes in the production of the senses.

The view of the *Vyāsa-bhāshya* is, I believe, now quite clear since we see that the mahat through the asmitā generates from the latter (as differentiations from it, though it itself exists as integrated in the mahat), the senses, and their corresponding gross elements.

Before proceeding further to trace the development of the bhūtādi on the tanmātric side, I think it is best to refer to the views about the supposed difference between the Yoga and the views of the Sāṃkhya works about the evolution of the categories. Now according to the Yoga view two parallel lines of evolution start from mahat, one of which develops into the ego, manas, the five cognitive and the five conative senses, while on the other side it develops into the five grosser elements through the five tanmātras which are directly produced from mahat through the medium ahaṃkāra.

Thus the view as found in the Yoga works may be tabulated thus :—

Prakrti
|
Mahat or Asmitāmātra
|
Asmitā — Tanmātras—5
|
Asmitā → 11 senses
Tanmātras—5 → 5 gross elements

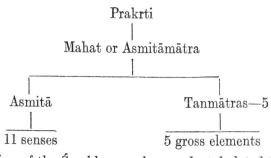

The view of the Śaṃkhya works may be tabulated thus :—

Prakṛti
|
Mahat
|
Ego
|
11 senses — 5 Tanmātras
|
5 Tanmātras → 5 gross elements

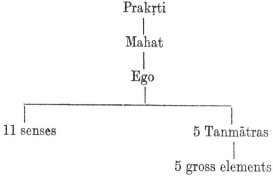

The place in the *Vyāsa-bhāshya* which refers to this genesis is that under *viśeshāviśeshaliṅgamātrāliṅgāni guṇaparvāṇi,* II. 19. There it says that the four bhūtas are ether, air, fire, water and earth. These are the viśeshas (specialised modifications) of the unspecialised modifications the tanmātras of sound, touch, colour, taste and smell. So also are the cognitive senses of hearing, touch, eye, tongue, and nose and the conative senses of speech, hand, feet, anus and the generative organ. The eleventh one manas (the co-ordinating organ) has for its object the objects of all the above ten senses. So these are the specialised modifications (*viśeshas*) of the unspecialised (aviśesha) asmitā. The guṇas have these sixteen kinds of specialised modifications (*viśeshapariṇāma*). The six unspecialised modifications are the sound tanmātra, touch tanmātra, colour tanmātra, taste tanmātra and smell tanmātra. These tanmātras respectively contain one, two, three, four, and five special characteristics. The sixth unspecialised modification is asmitāmātra. These are the six aviśesha evolutions of the pure being, the mahat. The category of mahat is merely a sign beyond the aviśeshas and it is there that these exist and develop.

In this *Vyāsa-bhāshya* the fully specialised ones, viśeshas, the grosser elements are said to have been derived from the tanmātras and the senses and manas, the faculty of reflection are said to have been specialised from the ego or asmitā. The tanmātras, however, have not been derived from the ego or asmitā here. But they together with asmitā are spoken of as the six slightly specialised ones, the five being the five tanmātras and the sixth one being the ego. These six aviśeshas are the specialisations of the mahat, the great egohood of pure Be-ness. It therefore appears that the six aviśeshas are directly derived from the mahat, after which the ego develops into the eleven senses and the tanmātras into the five gross elements in three different lines.

But let us see how *Yoga-vārttika* explains the point here :—

" But like the senses the tanmātras are also special modifications of the ahaṃkāra having specially modified characteristics such as sound, touch, etc., why, therefore, are they not mentioned as special modifications (*viśeshas*) ? The answer is that those only are mentioned as special modification which are ultimate special modifications. The tanmātras are indeed the special modifications of the ego, but they themselves produce further special modifications, the bhūtas. The aviśeshas are explained as the six aviśeshas. The tanmātras are generated from the tāmasa ahaṃkāra gradually through sound, etc. The category of mahat which is the ground of all modifications, called also the buddhi, has six evolutionary products called the aviśeshas. Though the mahat and the prakṛti may also be regarded as the root-causes out of which the tanmātras have evolved, yet the word aviśesha is used as a technical term having a special application to the six aviśeshas only." The modifications of these are from the buddhi through the intermediate stage of the ahaṃkāra, as has been explained in the *Bhāshya*, I. 45.

Thus we see that the *Yoga-vārttika* says that the *Bhāshya* is here describing the modifications of buddhi in two distinct classes, the aviśeshas and the viśeshas ; and that the mahat has been spoken of as the source of all the aviśeshas, the five tanmātras and the ego ; strictly speaking, however, the genesis of the tanmātras from mahat takes place through the ego and in association with the ego, for it has been so described in the *Bhāshya*, I. 45.

Nāgeśa in explaining this *Bhāshya* only repeats the view of *Yoga-vārttika.*

Now let us refer to the *Bhāshya* of I. 45, alluded to by the *Yoga-vārttika :* "The gradual series of subtler causes proceeds up to the aliṅga or the prakṛti. The earth atom has the smell tanmātra as its subtle cause ; the water atom has the taste tanmātra ; the air atom the touch tanmātra ; the ākāśa atom the sound tanmātra ; and of these ahaṃkāra is the subtle cause ; and of this the mahat is the subtle cause." Here by subtle cause (*sūkshma*) it is upādānakāraṇa or material cause which is meant ; so the *Bhāshya* further says : "It is true that purusha is the subtlest of all. But yet as prakṛti is subtler than the mahat, it is not in that sense that purusha is subtler than prakṛti for purusha is only an instrumental cause of the evolution of mahat, but not its material cause." I believe it is quite clear that ahaṃkāra is spoken of here as the *sūkshma anvayikārana* of the tanmātras. This anvayikāraṇa is the same as upādāna (material cause) as Vācaspati calls it. Now again in the *Bhāshya* of the same *sūtra* II. 19 later on we see the liṅga or the mahat is the stage next to prakṛti, it is differentiated from it though still remaining integrated in the regular order of evolution. The six aviśeshas are again differentiated while still remaining integrated in the mahat in the order of evolution (*pariṇāma-kramaniyama*).

The mahat tattva (liṅga) is associated with the prakṛti (aliṅga). Its development is thus to be considered as the production of a differentiation as integrated within the prakṛti. The six aviśeshas are also to be considered as the production of successive differentiations as integrated within the mahat.

The words *saṃsṛshṭa vivicyante* are the most important here for they show us the real nature of the transformations. "*Saṃsṛshtā*" means integrated and "*vivicyante*" means differentiated. This shows that the order of evolution as found in the Sāṃkhya works (viz. mahat from prakṛti, ahaṃkāra from mahat and the eleven senses and the tanmātras from ahaṃkāra) is true only in this sense that these modifications of ahaṃkāra take place directly as differentiations of characters in the body of mahat. As these differentiations take place through ahaṃkāra as the first moment in the series of transformations it is said that the transformations take place directly from ahaṃkāra; whereas when stress is laid on the other aspect it appears that the transformations are but differentiations as integrated in the body of the mahat, and thus it is also said that from mahat the six aviśeshas—namely, ahaṃkāra and the five tanmātras—come out. This conception of evolution as differentiation within integration bridges the gulf between the views of Yoga and the Saṃkhya works. We know that the tanmātras are produced from the tāmasa ahaṃkāra. This ahaṃkāra is nothing but the tāmasa side of mahat roused into creative activity by rajas.

The sāttvika ahaṃkāra is given as a separate category producing the senses, whereas the tamas as bhūtādi produces the tanmātras from its disturbance while held up within the mahat.*

Nāgeśa in the *Chāyā-vyākhyā* of II. 19, however, follows the Sāṃkhya explanation. He says : " The five tanmātras having in order one, two, three, four and five characteristics are such that the preceding ones are the causes of the succeeding ones. The śabdatanmātra has only the characteristic of sound, the sparśatanmātra of sound and touch and so on. . . . All these tanmātras are produced from the tāmasa ahaṃkāra in the order of śabda, sparśa, etc." This ignores the interpretation of the *Vyāsa-bhāshya* that the tanmātras are differentiations within the integrated whole of mahat through the intermediary stage of the tāmasa ahaṃkāra.

* This was first pointed out by Dr. B. N. Seal in his *Physical, Chemical and Mechanical Theories of the Ancient Hindus* in Dr. P. C. Ray's *Hindu Chemistry*, Vol. II.

CHAPTER VI

EVOLUTION AND CHANGE OF QUALITIES

THE order of the evolution of the tanmātras as here referred to is as follows :—

Bhūtādi (tāmasa ahaṃkāra)
|
Śabdatanmātra
|
Sparśatanmātra
|
Rūpatanmātra
|
Rasatanmātra
|
Gandhatanmātra

The evolution of the tanmātras has been variously described in the Purāṇas and the Smṛti literature. These divergent views can briefly be brought under two headings : those which derive the tanmātras from the bhûtas and those which derive them from the ahaṃkāra and the bhûtas from them. Some of these schools have been spoken of in the Barabara Muni's commentary on the *Tattvatraya*—a treatise on the Rāmānuja Philosophy—and have been already explained in a systematic way by Dr. B. N. Seal. I therefore refrain from repeating them needlessly. About the derivation of the tanmātras all the other Sāṃkhya treatises, the *Kārikā*, the *Kaumudī*, the *Tattvavaiśāradī*, the *Sūtra* and *Pravacana-bhāshya*, the

Siddhāntacandrikā, *Sūtrārthabodhinī*, the *Rajamārtaṇḍa* and the *Maṇiprabhā* seem to be silent. Further speaking of the tanmātras, Vijñāna Bhikshu says that the tanmātras exist only in unspecialised forms ; they therefore can be neither felt nor perceived in any way by the senses of ordinary men. This is that indeterminate state of matter in which they can never be distinguished one from the other, and they cannot be perceived to be possessed of different qualities or specialised in any way. It is for this that they are called tanmātras, i.e. their only specialization is a mere thatness. The Yogins alone perceive them.

Now turning towards the further evolution of the grosser elements from the tanmātras, we see that there are great divergences of view here also, some of which are shown below. Thus Vācaspati says : " The earth atom is produced from the five tanmātras with a predominance of the smell tanmātra, the water atom from the four tanmātras excepting the smell tanmātra with a preponderance of the taste tanmātra, and so on " (I. 44).

Thus here we find that the ākāśa atom (aṇu) has been generated simply by the ākāśa tanmātra ; the vāyu atom has been generated by two tanmātras, śabda and sparśa, of which the sparśa appears there as the chief. The tejas atom has been developed from the śabda, sparśa and rûpa tanmātras, though the rûpa is predominant in the group. The ap atom has been developed from the four tanmātras, śabda, sparśa, rûpa and rasa, though rasa is predominant in the group, and the earth or kshiti atom has been developed from the five tanmātras, though the gandha tanmātra is predominant in the group.

Now the *Yoga-vārttika* agrees with Vācaspati in all these details, but differs from him only in maintaining that the ākāśa atom has been generated from the śabda tanmātra with an accretion from bhūtādi, whereas Vācaspati says that the ākāśa atom is generated simply by the ākāśa tanmātra.*

Nāgeśa, however, takes a slihgtly different view and says that to produce the gross atoms from the tanmātras, an accretion of bhūtādi as an accompanying agent is necessary at every step ; so that we see that the vāyu atom is produced from these three : śabda + sparśa + accretion from bhūtādi. Tejas atom = śabda + śparśa + rūpa + accretion from bhūtādi. Ap atom = śabda + śparśa + rūpa + rasa + accretion from bhūtādi. Kshiti atom = śabda + śparśa + rūpa + rasa + gandha + accretion from bhūtādi.

I refrain from giving the *Vishṇu Purāṇa* view which has also been quoted in the *Yoga-vārttika*, and the view of a certain school of Vedāntists mentioned in the *Tattva-nirūpaṇa* and referred to and described in the *Tattvatraya*, as Dr. B. N. Seal has already described them in his article.

We see thus that from bhūtādi come the five tanmātras which can be compared to the Vaiśeshika atoms as they have no parts and neither grossness nor visible differentiation.† Some differentiation has of course already begun in the tanmātras, as they are called śabda, śparśa, rūpa, rasa and gandha, which therefore may be said to belong to a class akin to the grosser elements of ākāśa, vāyu, tejas, ap and kshiti.‡

The next one, the paramāṇu (atom), which is gross in its nature and is generated from the tanmātras which exist in it as parts (*tanmātrāvayava*) may be compared with the trasareṇu of the Vaiśeshikas. Thus the *Yoga-vārttika* says : "this is called paramāṇu by the Vaiśeshikas. We however call the subtlest part of the visible earth, earth atoms"

* *Yoga-vārttika*, I. 45.

† I have already said before that Bhikshu thinks that the guṇas (except the all-pervading ones) may be compared to the Vaiśeshika atoms. See *Yoga-vārttika*, III. 52.

‡ Cf. *Vyāsa-bhāshya*—"*sabdādīnāṃ mūrttisamānajâtīyānāṃ*," IV. 14.

(IV. 14). The doctrine of atoms is recognised both in the *Yoga-sūtrās* (I. 46) and the *Bhāshya* (III. 52, IV. 14, etc.). Whether Sāṃkhya admitted the paramāṇus (atoms) or not cannot be definitely settled. The *Sāṃkhya-kārikā* does not mention the paramāṇus, but Vijñāna Bhikshu thinks that the word "*sūkshma*" in *Kārikā*, 39, means paramāṇus (*Yoga-vārttika* IV. 14). Though the word paramāṇu is not mentioned in the *Kārikā*, I can hardly suppose that Sāṃkhya did not admit it in the sense in which Yoga did. For it does not seem probable that Sāṃkhya should think that by the combination of the subtle tanmātras we could all at once have the bigger lumps of bhūta without there being any particles. Moreover, since the Yoga paramāṇus are the finest visible particles of matter it could not have been denied by Sāṃkhya. The supposition of some German scholars that Sāṃkhya did not admit the paramāṇus does not seem very plausible. Bhikshu in *Yoga-vārttika*, III. 52, says that the guṇas are in reality Vaiśeshika atoms.

The third form is gross air, fire, water, etc., which is said to belong to the mahat (gross) class. I cannot express it better than by quoting a passage from *Yoga-vārttika*, IV. 4 : "The *Bhāshya* holds that in the tanmātras there exists the specific differentiation that constitutes the five tanmātras, the kshiti atom is generated and by the conglomeration of these gross atoms gross earth is formed. So again by the combination of the four tanmātras the water atom is formed and the conglomeration of these water atoms makes gross water."

"It should be noted here : since the *Bhāshya* holds that the tanmātras of sound, etc., are of the same class as the corresponding gross elements it may be assumed that the combining tanmātras possess the class characteristics which are made manifest in gross elements by hardness, smoothness, etc." Bhikshu holds that since Sāṃkhya and Yoga are similar (*samānatantra*) this is to be regarded as being also the Sāṃkhya view.

There is, however, another measure which is called the measure of parama mahat, which belongs to ākāśa for example.

Now these paramāṇus or atoms are not merely atoms of matter but they contain within themselves those particular qualities by virtue of which they appear, as pleasant, unpleasant or passive to us. If we have expressed ourselves clearly, I believe it has been shown that when the inner and the outer proceed from one source, the ego and the external world do not altogether differ in nature from the inner; both have been formed by the collocation of the guṇas (*sarvamidaṃ guṇānāṃ sanniveśaviseshamātram*). The same book which in the inner microcosm is written in the language of ideas has been in the external world written in the language of matter. So in the external world we have all the grounds of our inner experience, cognitive as well as emotional, pleasurable as well as painful. The modifications of the external world are only translated into ideas and feelings; therefore these paramāṇus are spoken of as endowed with feelings.

There is another difference between the tanmātras and the paramāṇus. The former cannot be perceived to be endowed with the feeling elements as the latter. Some say, however, that it is not true that the tanmātras are not endowed with the feeling elements, but they cannot be perceived by any save the Yogins; thus it is said: *tanmātrāṇāmapi parasparavyāvṛttasvabhāvatvamastyeva tacca yogimātragamyam.* The tanmātras also possess differentiated characters, but they can be perceived only by the Yogins; but this is not universally admitted.

Now these paramāṇus cannot further be evolved into any other different kind of existence or tattvāntara.* We see that the paramāṇus though they have been formed from the tanmātras resemble them only in a very remote way and are therefore placed in a separate stage of evolution.

* *Vyāsa-bhāshya*, II. 19.

With the bhūtas we have the last stage of evolution of the guṇas. The course of evolution, however, does not cease here, but continues ceaselessly, though by its process no new stage of existence is generated, but the product of the evolution is such that in it the properties of the gross elements which compose its constitution can be found directly. This is what is called *dharmapariṇāma*, as distinguished from the *tattvāntara-pariṇāma* spoken above. The evolution of the viśeshas from the aviśeshas is always styled tattvāntara-pariṇāma, as opposed to the evolution that takes place among the viśeshas themselves, which is called *dharmapariṇāma* or evolution by change of qualities. Now these atoms or paramāṇus of kshiti, ap, tejas, marut or ākāśa conglomerate together and form all sentient or non-sentient bodies in the world. The different atoms of earth, air, fire, water, etc., conglomerate together and form the different animate bodies such as cow, etc., or inanimate bodies such as jug, etc., and vegetables like the tree, etc. These bodies are built up by the conglomerated units of the atoms in such a way that they are almost in a state of combination which has been styled *ayutasiddhāvayava*. In such a combination the parts do not stand independently, but only hide themselves as it were in order to manifest the whole body, so that by the conglomeration of the particles we have what may be called a body, which is regarded as quite a different thing from the atoms of which it is composed. These bodies change with the different sorts of change or arrangement of the particles, according to which the body may be spoken of as "one," "large," "small," "tangible" or "possessing" the quality of action. Some philosophers hold the view that a body is really nothing but the conglomeration of the atoms; but they must be altogether wrong here since they have no right to ignore the "body," which appears before them with all its specific qualities and attributes; moreover, if they ignore the body they have to ignore almost everything, for the atoms themselves are not visible.

Again, these atoms, though so much unlike the Vaiśeshika atoms since they contain tanmātras of a different nature as their constituents and thus differ from the simpler atoms of the Vaiśeshikas, compose the constituents of all inorganic, organic or animal bodies in such a way that there is no break of harmony—no opposition between them;—but, on the contrary, when any one of the guṇas existing in the atoms and their conglomerations becomes prominent, the other guṇas though their functions are different from it, yet do not run counter to the prominent guṇas, but conjointly with them, help to form the specific modification for the experiences of the purusha. In the production of a thing, the different guṇas do not choose different independent courses for their evolution, but join together and effectuate themselves in the evolution of a single product. Thus we see also that when the atoms of different gross elements possessing different properties and attributes coalesce, their difference of attributes does not produce confusion, but they unite in the production of the particular substances by a common teleological purpose (see *Vyāsa-bhāshya*, IV. 14).

We thus see that the bodies or things composed by the collocation of the atoms in one sense differ from the atoms themselves and in another are identical with the atoms themselves. We see therefore that the appearance of the atoms as bodies or things differs with the change of position of the atoms amongst themselves. So we can say that the change of the appearance of things and bodies only shows the change of the collocation of the atoms, there being always a change of appearance in the bodies consequent on every change in the position of the atoms. The former therefore is only an explicit appearance of the change that takes place in the substance itself; for the appearance of a thing is only an explicit aspect of the very selfsame thing—the atoms; thus the *Bhāshya* says: *dharmisvarūpamātro hi dharmaḥ, dharmivrikriyā eva eshā dharmadvārā prapañcyate,* i.e. a dharma (quality) is merely the nature of the dharmin (substance), and it is the changes of the dharmin that are made explicit by the dharmas.* Often it happens that the change of appearance of a thing or a body, a tree or a piece of cloth, for example, can be marked only after a long interval. This, however, only shows that the atoms of the body had been continually changing and consequently the appearance of the body or the thing also had been continually changing; for otherwise we can in no way account for the sudden change of appearance. All bodies are continually changing the constituent collocation of atoms and their appearances. In the smallest particle of time or kshaṇa the whole universe undergoes a change. Each moment or the smallest particle of time is only the manifestation of that particular change. Time therefore has not a separate existence in this philosophy as in the Vaiśeshika, but it is only identical with the smallest amount of change—viz. that of an atom of its own amount of space. Now here the appearance is called the dharma, and that particular arrangement of atoms or guṇas which is the basis of the particular appearance is called the dharmin. The change of appearance is therefore called the dharma-pariṇāma.†

Again this change of appearance can be looked at from two other aspects which though not intrinsically different from the change of appearance have their own special points of view which make them remarkable. These are *lakshaṇa-pariṇāma* and *avasthā-pariṇāma*. Taking the particular collocation of atoms in a body for review, we see that all the subsequent changes that take place in it exist in it only in a latent way in it which will be manifested in future. All the previous

* *Vyāsa-bhāshya,* III. 13. † *Ibid.*

changes of the collocating atoms are not also lost but exist only in a sublatent way in the particular collocation of atoms present before us. For the past changes are by no means destroyed but are preserved in the peculiar and particular collocation of atoms of the present moment. For had not the past changes taken place, the present could not appear. The present had held itself hidden in the past just as the future is hidden within the present. It therefore only comes into being with the unfolding of the past, which therefore exists only in a sublatent form in it.

It is on account of this that we see that a body comes into being and dies away. Though this birth or death is really subsumed the change of appearance yet it has its own special aspect, on account of which it has been given a separate name as lakshaṇa-pariṇāma. It considers the three stages of an appearance—the unmanifested when it exists in the future, the manifested moment of the present, and the past when it has been manifested—lost to view but preserved and retained in all the onward stages of the evolution. Thus when we say that a thing has not yet come into being, that it has just come into being, and that it is no longer, we refer to this lakshaṇa-pariṇāma which records the history of the thing in future, present and past, which are only the three different moments of the same thing according to its different characters, as unmanifested, manifested and manifested in the past but conserved.

Now it often happens that though the appearance of a thing is constantly changing owing to the continual change of the atoms that compose it, yet the changes are so fine and infinitesimal that they cannot be marked by anyone except the Yogins ; for though structural changes may be going on tending towards the final passing away of that structure and body into another structure and body, which greatly differs from it, yet they may not be noticed by us, who can take note of the bigger changes alone. Taking therefore two remarkable stages of things, the difference between which may be so notable as to justify us in calling the later the dissolution or destruction of the former, we assert that the thing has suffered growth and decay in the interval, during which the actual was passing into the sublatent and the potential was tending towards actualization. This is what is called the avasthā-pariṇāma, or change of condition, which, however, does not materially differ from the lakshaṇa-pariṇāma and can thus be held to be a mode of it. It is on account of this that a substance is called new or old, grown or decayed. Thus in explaining the illustration given in the *Bhāshya*, III. 13 : "there is avasthā-pariṇāma. At the moments of cessation the potencies of cessation become stronger and those of ordinary experience weaker." The *Yoga-vārttika* says : "The strength and weakness of the two potencies is like the newness or oldness of a jug ; growth and decay being the same as origination and decease, there is no difference here from *lakshaṇa-pariṇāma*."

It is now time for us to examine once more the relation of dharmin, substance, and dharma, its quality or appearance.

Dharmin, or substance, is that which remains common to the latent (as having passed over or *śānta*), the rising (the present or *udita*) and the unpredicable (future or *avyapadeśya*) characteristic qualities of the substance.

Substance (take for example, earth) has the power of existing in the form of particles of dust, a lump or a jug by which water may be carried. Now taking the stage of lump for examination we may think of its previous stage, that of particles of dust, as being latent, and its future stage as jug as the unpredicable. The earth we see here to be common to all these three stages which have come into being by its own activity and consequent changes. Earth here is the common quality which remains unchanged in all these stages, and so relatively constant among its changes as particles, lump and jug. This earth therefore is regarded as the dharmin, characterised one, the substance; and its stages as its dharma or qualities. When this dharmin, or substance, undergoes a change from a stage of lump to a stage of jug, it undergoes what is called *dharma-pariṇāma* or change of quality.

But its dharma, as the shape of the jug may be thought to have itself undorgone a change—inasmuch as it has now come into being, from a state of relative non-being, latency or unpredicability. This is called the lakshaṇa-pariṇāma of the dharma or qualities as constituting a jug. This jug is again suffering another change as new or old according as it is just produced or is gradually running towards its dissolution, and this is called the avasthā-pariṇāma or change of condition. These three, however, are not separate from the dharma-pariṇāma, but are only aspects of it; so it may be said that the dharmin or substance directly suffers the dharma-pariṇāma and indirectly the lakshaṇa and the avasthā-pariṇāma. The dharma, however, changes and the lakshaṇa-pariṇāma can be looked at from another point of view, that of change of state, viz. growth and decay. Thus we see that though the atoms of kshiti, ap, etc., remain unchanged, they are constantly suffering changes from the inorganic to plants and animals, and from thence again back to the inorganic. There is thus a constant circulation of changes in which the different atoms of kshiti, ap, tejas, vāyu and ākāśa remaining themselves unchanged are suffering dharma-pariṇāma as they are changed from the inorganic to plants and animals and back again to the inorganic. These different states or dharmas (as inorganic, etc.), again, according as they are not yet, now, or no longer or passed over, are suffering the lakshaṇa-pariṇāma. There is also the avasthā-pariṇāma of these states according as any one of them (the plant state for example) is growing or suffering decay towards its dissolution.

This circulation of cosmic matter in general applies also to all particular things, such as the jug, the cloth, etc.; the order of evolution here will be that of powdered particles of earth, lump of earth, the earthen jug, the broken halves of the jug, and again the powdered earth. As the whole substance has only one identical evolution, these different states only happen in order of succession, the occurrence of one characteristic being displaced by another characteristic which comes after it immediately. We thus see that one substance may undergo endless changes of characteristic in order of succession; and along with the change of characteristic or dharma we have the lakshaṇa-pariṇāma and the avasthā-pariṇāma as old or new, which is evidently one of infinitesimal changes of growth and decay. Thus Vācaspati gives the following beautiful example: "Even the most carefully preserved rice in the granary becomes after long years so brittle that it crumbles into atoms. This change cannot happen to new rice all on a sudden. Therefore we have to admit an order of successive changes" (*Tattvavaivśāradī*, III. 15).

We now see that substance has neither past nor future; appearances or qualities only are manifested in time, by virtue of which substance is also spoken of as varying and changing temporally, just as a line remains unchanged in itself but acquires different significances according as one or two zeros are placed on its right side. Substance—the atoms of kshiti, ap, tejas, marut, vyoman, etc., by various changes of quality appear as the manifold varieties of cosmical existence. There is no intrinsic difference between one thing and another, but only changes of character of one and the same thing; thus the gross elemental atoms like water and earth particles acquire various qualities and appear as the various juices of all fruits and herbs. Now in analogy with the arguments stated above, it will seem that even a qualified thing or appearance may be relatively regarded as substance, when it is seen to remain common to various other modifications of that appearance itself. Thus a jug, which may remain common in all its modifications of colour, may be regarded relatively as the dharmin or substance of all these special appearances or modifications of the same appearance.

We remember that the guṇas, which are the final substratum of all the grosser particles, are always in a state of commotion and always evolving in the manner previously stated, for the sake of the experience and final realisation of the parusha, the only object or end of the prakṛti. Thus the *Bhāshya*, III. 13, says: "So it is the nature of the guṇas that there cannot remain even a moment without the evolutionary changes of dharma, lakshaṇa and avasthā; movement is the characteristic of the guṇas. The nature of the guṇas is the cause of their constant movement."

Although the pioneers of modern scientific evolution have tried to observe scientifically some of the stages of the growth of the inorganic and of the animal worlds into the man, yet they do not give any reason for it. Theirs is more an experimental assertion of facts than a metaphysical account of evolution. According to Darwin the general form of the evolutionary process is that which is accomplished by "very slight variations which are accumulated by the effect of natural selection." And according to a later theory, we see that a new species is constituted all at once by the simultaneous appearance of several new characteristics very different from the old. But why this accidental variation, this seeming departure from the causal chain, comes into being, the evolutionists cannot explain. But the Sāṃkhya-Pātañjala doctrine explains it from the standpoint of teleology or the final goal inherent in all matter, so that it may be serviceable to the purusha. To be serviceable to the purusha is the one moral purpose in all prakṛti and its manifestations in the whole material world, which guide the course and direction of the smallest particle of matter. From the scientific point of view, the Sāṃkhya-Pātañjala doctrine is very much in the same position as modern science, for it does not explain the cause of the accidental variation noticed in all the stages of evolutionary process from any physical point of view based on the observation of facts.

But it does much credit to the Pātañjala doctrines that they explain this accidental variation, this *avyapadeśyatva* or unpredicability of the onward course of evolution from a moral point of view, that of teleology, the serviceability of the purusha. They found, however, that this teleology should not be used to usurp the whole nature and function of matter. We find that the atoms are always moving by virtue of the rajas or energy, and it is to this movement of the atoms in space that all the products of evolution are due. We have found that the difference between the juices of Coco-nut, Palm, Bel, Tinduka (Diospyros Embryopteries), Āmalaka (Emblic Myrobalan) can be accounted for by the particular and peculiar arrangement of the atoms of earth and water alone, by their stress and strain; and we see also that the evolution of the organic from the inorganic is due to this change of position of the atoms themselves; for the unit of change is the change in an atom of its own dimension of spatial position. There is always the transformation of energy from the inorganic to the organic and back again from the organic. Thus the differences among things are solely due to the different stages which they occupy in the scale of evolution, as different expressions of the transformation of energy; but virtually there is no intrinsic difference among things *sarvaṃ sarvātmakaṃ*; the change of the collocation of atoms only changes potentiality into actuality, for there is potentiality of everything for every thing everywhere throughout this changing world.

Thus Vācaspati writes: "The water possessing taste, colour, touch and sound and the earth possessing smell, taste, colour, touch, and sound suffer an infinite variety of changes as roots, flowers, fruits, leaves and their specific tastes and other qualities. The water and the earth which do not possess these qualities cannot have them, for we have proved that what is non-existent cannot come into being. The trees and plants produce the varied tastes and colours in animals, for it is by eating these that they acquire such richness of colour, etc. Animal products can again produce changes in plant bodies. By sprinkling blood on it a pomegranate may be made as big as a palm" (*Tattvavaiśaradī*, III. 14).

Looked at from the point of view of the guṇas, there is no intrinsic difference between things, though there are a thousand manifestations of differences, according to time, place, form and causality. The expressions of the guṇas, and the manifestations of the transformations of energy differ according to time, place, shape, or causality—these are the determining circumstances and environments which determine the modes of the evolutionary process; surrounding environments are also involved in determining this change, and it is said that two Āmalaka fruits placed in two different places undergo two different sorts of changes in connection with the particular spots in which they are placed, and that if anybody interchanges them a Yogin can recognise and distinguish the one from the other by seeing the changes that the fruits have undergone in connection with their particular points of space. Thus the *Bhāshya* says: "Two Āmalaka fruits having the same characteristic genus and species, their situation in two different points of space contributes to their specific distinction of development, so that they may be identified as this and that. When an Āmalaka is brought from a distance to a man previously inattentive to it, he naturally cannot distinguish this Āmalaka as being the distant one which has been brought before him without his knowledge. But right knowledge should be competent to discern the distinction; and the sūtra says that the place associated with one Āmalaka fruit is different from the place associated with another Āmalaka at another point of space; and the Yogin can perceive the difference of their specific evolution in association with their points of space; similarly the atoms also suffer different modifications at different points of space which can be perceived by Īśvara and the Yogins" (*Vyāsa-bhāshya*, III. 53).

Vācaspati again says: "Though all cause is essentially all effects yet a particular cause takes effect in a particular place, thus though the cause is the same, yet saffron grows in Kāśmīra and not in Pāñcāla. So, the rains do not come in summer, the vicious do not enjoy happiness. Thus in accordance with the obstructions of place, time, animal form, and instrumental accessories, the same cause does not produce the same effect. Though as cause everything is essentially everything else, yet there is a particular country for a particular effect, such as Kāśmīra is for saffron. Even though the causes may be in other countries such as Pāñcāla, yet the effect will not happen there, and for this reason saffron does not manifest itself in Pāñcāla. So in summer there are no rains and so no paddy grows then" (*Tattvavaiśāradī*, III. 14).

We see therefore that time, space, etc., are the limitations which regulate, modify and determine to a certain extent the varying transformations and changes and the seeming differences of things, though in reality they are all ultimately reducible to the three guṇas; thus Kāśmīra being the country of saffron, it will not grow in the Pāñcāla country, even though the other causes of its growth should all be present there;—here the operation of cause is limited by space.

After considering the inorganic, vegetable and animal kingdoms as three stages in the evolutionary process, our attention is at once drawn to their conception of the nature of relation of plant life to animal life. Though I do not find any special reference in the *Bhāshya* to this point, yet I am reminded of a few passages in the *Mahābhārata*, which I think may be added as a supplement to the general doctrine of evolution according to the Sāṃkhya-Pātañjala philosophy as stated here. Thus the *Mahābhārata* says: "Even the solid trees have ether (ākāśa) in them which justifies the regular appearance of flowers and fruits. By heat the leaves, the bark, flowers and fruits become withered, and since there is withering and decay in them, there is in them the sensation of touch. Since by the sound of air, fire and thunder the fruits and flowers fall away, there must be the sense of hearing in them. The creepers encircle the trees and they go in all directions, and since without sight there could not be any choice of direction, the trees have the power of vision. By various holy and unholy smells and incenses of various kinds the trees are cured of their diseases and blossom forth, therefore the trees can smell. Since they drink by their roots, and since they get diseases, and since their diseases can be cured, there is the sense of taste in the trees. Since they enjoy pleasure and suffer pain, and since their parts which are cut grow, I see life everywhere in trees and not want of life" (*Śāntiparva*, 184).

Nīlakaṇṭha in his commentary goes still further and says that a hard substance called vajramaṇi also may be called living. Here we see that the ancients had to a certain extent forestalled the discovery of Sir J. C. Bose that the life functions differed only in degree between the three classes, the inorganic, plants and animals.

These are all, however, only illustrations of dharma-pariṇāma, for here there is no radical change in the elements themselves, the appearance of qualities being due only to the different arrangement of the atoms of the five gross elements. This change applies to the viśeshas only—the five gross elements externally and the eleven senses internally. How the inner microcosm, the manas and the senses are affected by dharma-pariṇāma we shall see hereafter, when we deal with the psychology of the Sāṃkhya-Pātañjala doctrine. For the present it will suffice to say that the citta or mind also suffers this change and is modified in a twofold mode ; the patent in the form of the ideas and the latent, as the substance itself, in the form of saṃskāras of subconscious impressions. Thus the *Bhāshya* says : "The mind has two kinds of characteristics, perceived and unperceived. Those of the nature of ideas are perceived and those inherent in the integral nature of it are unperceived. The latter are of seven kinds and may be ascertained by inference. These are cessation of mental states by samādhi, virtue and vice, subconscious impressions, change, life-functioning, power of movement, and energy" (III. 15).

This dharma-pariṇāma as we have shown it, is essentially different from the satkāraṇavāda of the aviśeshas described above. We cannot close this discussion about evolution without noticing the Sāṃkhya view of causation.

We have seen that the Sāṃkhya-Pātañjala view holds that the effect is already existent in the cause, but only in a potential form. "The grouping or collocation alone changes, and this brings out the manifestation of the latent powers of the guṇas, but without creation of anything absolutely new or non-existent." This is the true satkāryyavāda theory as distinguished from the so-called satkāryyavāda theory of the Vedāntists, which ought more properly to be called the satkāraṇavāda theory, for with them the cause alone is true, and all effects are illusory, being only impositions on the cause. For with them the material cause alone is true, whilst all its forms and shapes are merely illusory, whereas according to the Sāṃkhya-Pātañjala doctrine all the appearances or effects are true and are due to the power which the substance has of transforming itself into those various appearances and effects *yogyatāvacchinnā dharmiṇaḥ śaktireva dharmaḥ* (III. 14). The operation of the concomitant condition or efficient cause serves only to effect the passage of a thing from potency to actualisation.

Everything in the phenomenal world is but a special collocation of the guṇas; so that the change of collocation explains the diversity of things. Considered from the point of view of the guṇas, things are all the same, so excluding that, the cause of the diversity in things is the power which the guṇas have of changing their particular collocations and thus assuming various shapes. We have seen that the prakṛti unfolds itself through various stages—the mahat called the great being—the ahaṃkāra, the tanmātras called the aviśeshas. Now the liṅga at once resolves itself into the ahaṃkāra and through it again into the tanmātras. The ahaṃkāra and the tanmātras again resolve themselves into the senses and the gross elements, and these again are constantly suffering thousands of modifications called the dharma, lakshaṇa, and avasthā-pariṇāma according to the definite law of evolution (*pariṇāmakramaniyama*).

Now according to the Saṃkhya-Pātañjala doctrine, the śakti—power, force—and the śaktimān—the possessor of power or force—are not different but identical. So the prakṛti and all its emanations and modifications are of the nature of substantive entities as well as power or force. Their appearances as substantive entities and as power or force are but two aspects, and so it will be erroneous to make any such distinction as the substantive entity and its power or force. That which is the substantive entity is the force, and that which is the force is the substantive entity. Of course for all practical purposes we can indeed make some distinction, but that distinction is only relatively true. Thus when we say that earth is the substantive entity and the power which it has of transforming itself into the produced form, lump, or jug as its attribute, we see on the one hand that no distinction is really made between the appearance of the earth as jug and its power of transforming itself into the jug. As this power of transforming itself into lump or jug, etc., always abides in the earth we say that the jug, etc., are also abiding in the earth ; when the power is in the potential state, we say that the jug is in the potential state, and when it is actualised, we say that the jug has been actualised. Looked at from the tanmātric side, the earth and all the other gross elements must be said to be mere modifications, and as such identical with the power which the tanmātras have of changing themselves into them. The potentiality or actuality of any state is the mere potentiality or actuality of the power which its antecedent cause has of transforming itself into it.

CHAPTER VII

EVOLUTION AND CHANGE OF QUALITIES

PRAKṚTI, though a substantive entity is yet a potential power, being actualised as its various modifications, the aviśeshas and the viśeshas. Being of the nature of power, the movement by which it actualises itself is immanent within itself and not caused from without. The operation of the concomitant conditions is only manifested in the removal of the negative barriers by which the power was stopped or prevented from actualising itself. Being of the nature of power, its potentiality means that it is kept in equilibrium by virtue of the opposing tendencies inherent within it, which serve to obstruct one another and are therefore called the āvaraṇa śakti. Of course it is evident that there is no real or absolute distinction between the opposing force (*avaraṇa śakti*) and the energising force (*kāryyakarī śakti*); they may be called so only relatively, for the same tendency which may appear as the *āvaraṇa śakti* of some tendencies may appear as the *kāryyakarī śakti* elsewhere. The example chosen to explain the nature of prakṛti and its modifications conceived as power tending towards actuality from potentiality in the *Vyāsa-bhāshya* is that of a sheet of water enclosed by temporary walls within a field, but always tending to run out of it. As soon as the temporary wall is broken in some direction, the water rushes out of itself, and what one has to do is to break the wall at a particular place. Prakṛti is also the potential for all the infinite diversity of things in the phenomenal world, but the potential tendency of all these mutually opposed and diverse things cannot be actualised together. Owing to the concomitant conditions when the barrier of a certain tendency is removed, it at once actualises itself in its effect and so on.

We can only expect to get any effect from any cause if the necessary barriers can be removed, for everything is everything potentially and it is only necessary to remove the particular barrier which is obstructing the power from actualising itself in that particular effect towards which it is always potentially tending. Thus Nandī who was a man is at once turned into a god for his particular merit, which served to break all the barriers of the potential tendency of his body towards becoming divine, so that the barriers being removed the potential power of the prakṛti of his body at once actualises itself in the divine body.

The *Vyāsa-bhāshya* (III. 14) mentions four sorts of concomitant conditions which can serve to break the barrier in a particular way and thus determine the mode or form of the actualisations of the potential. These are (1) ākāra, form and constitution of a thing ; deśa, place, (3) kāla, time ; thus from a piece of stone, the shoot of a plant cannot proceed, for the arrangement of the particles in stone is such that it will oppose and stand as a bar to its potential tendencies to develop into the shoot of a plant ; of course if these barriers could be removed, say by the will of God, as Vijñāna Bhikshu says, then it is not impossible that the shoot of a plant might grow from a stone. By the will of God poison may be turned into nectar and nectar into poison, and there is no absolute certainty of the course of the evolutionary process, for God's will can make any change in the direction of its process (*avyavasthitākhilapariṇāmo bhavatyeva*, III. 14).

According to the Sāṃkhya-Pātañjala theory dharma, merit, can only be said to accrue from those actions which lead to a man's salvation, and adharma from just the opposite course of conduct. When it is said that these can remove the barriers of the prakṛti and thus determine its modifications, it amounts almost to saying that the modifications of the prakṛti are being regulated by the moral conditions of man. According to the different stages of man's moral evolution, different kinds of merit, dharma or adharma, accrue, and these again regulate the various physical and mental phenomena according to which a man may be affected either pleasurably or painfully. It must, however, be always remembered that the dharma and adharma are also the productions of prakṛti, and as such cannot affect it except by behaving as the cause for the removal of the opposite obstructions—the dharma for removing the obstructions of adharma and adharma for those of dharma. Vijñāna Bhikshu and Nāgeśa agree here in saying that the modifications due to dharma and adharma are those which affect the bodies and senses. What they mean is possibly this, that it is dharma or adharma alone which guides the transformations of the bodies and senses of all living beings in general and the Yogins.

The body of a person and his senses are continually decaying and being reconstructed by refilling from the gross elements and from ahaṃkāra respectively. These refillings proceed automatically and naturally; but they follow the teleological purpose as chalked out by the law of karma in accordance with the virtues or vices of a man. Thus the gross insult to which the sages were subjected by Nahusha* was so effective a sin that by its influence the refilling of Nahusha's body and the senses was stopped and the body and senses of a snake were directly produced by a process of refilling from the gross elements and ahaṃkāra, for providing him with a body in which he could undergo the sufferings which were his due owing to the enormity of his vice. Thus by his vicious action

* Nahusha an earthly king became Indra the king of the gods by the fruition of his virtues, but on account of gross misdeeds fell from Heaven and was turned into a snake.

the whole machinery of prakṛti was set in operation so that he at once died and was immediately reborn as a snake. In another place Vācaspati "the virtuous enjoys happiness" as an illustration of the cause of dharma and adharma as controlling the course of the development of prakṛti. We therefore see that the sphere of merit and demerit lies in the helping of the formation of the particular bodies and senses (from the gross elements and ahaṃkāra respectively) suited to all living beings according to their stages of evolution and their growth, decay, or other sorts of their modifications as pleasure, pain, and also as illness or health. Thus it is by his particular merit that the Yogin can get his special body or men or animals can get their new bodies after leaving the old ones at death. Thus *Yoga-vārttika* says: "Merit by removing the obstructions of demerit causes the development of the body and the senses."

As for Īśvara I do not remember that the *Bhāshya* or the sūtras ever mention Him as having anything to do with the controlling of the modifications of the prakṛti by removing the barriers, but all the later commentators agree in holding him responsible for the removal of all barriers in the way of prakṛtis development. So that Īśvara is the root cause of all the removal of barriers, including those that are affected by merit and demerit. Thus Vācaspati says (IV. 3): *Īśvarasyāpi dharmādhishṭhānārthaṃ pratibandhāpanaya eva vyāpāro*, i.e. God stands as the cause of the removal of such obstacles in the prakṛti as may lead to the fruition of merit or demerit.

Yoga-vārttika and Nāgeśa agree in holding Īśvara responsible for the removal of all obstacles in the way of the evolution of prakṛti. Thus Bhikshu says that God rouses prakṛti by breaking the opposing forces of the state of equilibrium and also of the course of evolution (IV. 3).

It is on account of God that we can do good or bad actions and thus acquire merit or demerit. Of course God is not active and cannot cause any motion in prakṛti. But He by His very presence causes the obstacles, as the barriers in the way of prakṛti's development, to be removed, in such a way that He stands ultimately responsible for the removal of all obstacles in the way of prakṛti's development and thus also of all obstacles in the way of men's performance of good or bad deeds. Man's good or bad deeds "puṇyakarma," apuṇya-arma, dharma or adharma serve to remove the obstacles of prakṛti in such a way as to result in pleasurable or painful effects; but it is by God's help that the barriers of prakṛti are removed and it yields itself in such a way that a man may perform good or bad deeds according to his desire. Nīlakaṇṭha, however, by his quotations in explanation of 300/2, *Śāntiparva*, leads us to suppose that he regards God's will as wholly responsible for the performance of our good or bad actions. For if we lay stress on his quotation "He makes him do good deeds whom He wants to raise, and He makes him commit bad deeds whom He wants to throw down," it appears that he whom God wants to raise is made to perform good actions and he whom God wants to throw downwards is made to commit bad actions. But this seems to be a very bold idea, as it will altogether nullify the least vestige of freedom in and responsibility for our actions and is unsupported by the evidence of other commentators. Vijñāna Bhikshu also says with reference to this śruti in his *Vijñānamṛta-bhāshya*, III. 33: "As there is an infinite *regressus* between the causal connection of seed and shoot, so one karma is being determined by the previous karma and so on; there is no beginning to this chain." So we take the superintendence of merits and demerits (*dharm-ādhispṭhānatā*) by Īśvara to mean only in a general way the help that is offered by Him in removing the obstructions of the external world in such a manner that it may be possible for a man to perform practically meritorious acts in the external world.

Nīlakaṇṭha commenting on the Yoga view says that "like a piece of magnet, God though inactive, may by His very presence stir up prakṛti and help His devotees. So the Yoga holds that for the granting of emancipation God has to be admitted" (*Śāntiparva*, 300/2).

In support of our view we also find that it is by God's influence that the unalterable nature of the external world is held fast and a limit imposed on the powers of man in producing changes in the external world. Thus Vācaspati in explaining the Bhāshya (III. 45) says: "Though capable of doing it, yet he does not change the order of things, because another earlier omnipotent being had wished the things to be such as they were. They would not disobey the orders of the omnipotent God."

Men may indeed acquire unlimited powers of producing any changes they like, for the powers of objects as they change according to the difference of class, space, time and condition, are not permanent, and so it is proper that they should act in accordance with the desire of the Yogin; but there is a limit to men's will by the command of God—thus far and no further.

Another point in our favour is that the Yoga philosophy differs from the Sāṃkhya mainly in this that the purushārtha or serviceability to the purusha is only the aim or end of the evolution of prakṛti and not actually the agent which removes the obstacles of the prakṛti in such a way as to determine its course as this cosmical process of evolution. Purushārtha is indeed the aim for which the process of evolution exists; for this manifold evolution in its entirety affects the interests of the purusha alone; but that does not prove that its teleology can really guide the evolution on its particular lines so as to ensure the best possible mode of serving all the interests of the purusha, for this teleology being immanent in the prakṛti is essentially non-intelligent. Thus Vācaspati says: "The fulfilment of the purpose of the purusha is not also the prime mover. God has the fulfilment of the purpose of the purusha as His own purpose, for which He behaves as the prime mover. The fulfilment of the purpose of the purusha may be regarded as cause only in the sense that it is the object in view of God, the prime mover."*

The Sāṃkhya, however, hopes that this immanent purpose in prakṛti acts like a blind instinct and is able to guide the course of its evolution in all its manifold lines in accordance with the best possible service of the purusha.

The Pātañjala view, as we have seen, maintains that Īśvara removes all obstacles of prakṛti in such a way that this purpose may find scope for its realisation. Thus *Sūtrārtha-bodhinī*, IV. 3, of Nārāyaṇa Tīrtha says: "According to atheistic Sāṃkhya the future serviceability of purusha alone is the mover of prakṛti. But with us theists the serviceability of purusha is the object for which prakṛti moves. It is merely as an object that the serviceability of the purusha may be said to be the mover of the prakṛti."

As regards the connection of prakṛti and purusha, however, both Sāṃkhya and Pātañjala agree according to Vijñāna Bhikshu in denying the interference of Īśvara; it is the movement of prakṛti by virtue of immanent purpose that connects itself naturally with the purusha. Vijñāna Bhikshu's own view, however, is that this union is brought about by God (*Vijñānāmṛta-bhāshya*, p. 34).

To recapitulate, we see that there is an immanent purpose in prakṛti which connects it with the purushas. This purpose is, however, blind and cannot choose the suitable lines of development and cause the movement of Prakṛti along them for its fullest realisation. Prakṛti itself, though a substantial entity, is also essentially of the nature of conserved energy existing in the potential form but always ready to flow out

* *Tattravaiśāradī*, IV, 3.

and actualise itself, if only its own immanent obstructions are removed. Its teleological purpose is powerless to remove its own obstruction. God by His very presence removes the obstacles, by which, prakṛti of itself moves in the evolutionary process, and thus the purpose is realised ; for the removal of obstacles by the influence of God takes place in such a way that the purpose may realise its fullest scope. Realisation of the teleology means that the interests of purusha are seemingly affected and purusha appears to see and feel in a manifold way, and after a long series of such experiences it comes to understand itself in its own nature, and this being the last and final realisation of the purpose of prakṛti with reference to that purusha all connections of prakṛti with such a purusha at once cease ; the purusha is then said to be liberated and the world ceases for him to exist, though it exists for the other unliberated purushas, the purpose of the prakṛti with reference to whom has not been realised. So the world is both eternal and non-eternal, i.e. its eternality is only relative and not absolute. Thus the *Bhāshya* says the question " whether the world will have an end or not cannot be directly answered. The world-process gradually ceases for the wise and not for others, so no one-sided decision can be true " (IV. 33).

BOOK II. ETHICS AND PRACTICE

CHAPTER VIII

MIND AND MORAL STATES

THE Yoga philosophy has essentially a practical tone and its object consists mainly in demonstrating the means of attaining salvation, oneness, the liberation of the purusha. The metaphysical theory which we have discussed at some length, though it is the basis which justifies its ethical goal, is not itself the principal subject of Yoga discussion, and is only dealt with to the extent that it can aid in demonstrating the ethical view. We must now direct our attention to these ethical theories. Citta or mind always exists in the form of its states which are called vṛttis.* These comprehend all the manifold states of consciousness of our phenomenal existence. We cannot distinguish states of consciousness from consciousness itself, for the consciousness is not something separate from its states; it exists in them, passes away with their passing and submerges when they are submerged. It differs from the senses in this, that they represent the functions and faculties, whereas citta stands as the entity containing the conscious states with which we are directly concerned. But the citta which we have thus described as existing only in its states is called the kāryyacitta or citta as effect as distin-

* I have translated both citta and buddhi as mind. The word buddhi is used when emphasis is laid on the intellective and cosmical functions of the mind. The word citta is used when emphasis is laid on the conservative side of mind as the repository of all experiences, memory, etc.

guished from the kāraṇacitta or citta as cause. These kāraṇacittas or cittas as cause are all-pervading like the ākāśa and are infinite in number, each being connected with each of the numberless purushas or souls (*Chāyāvyākhyā*, IV. 10). The reason assigned for acknowledging such a kāraṇacitta which must be all pervading, as is evident from the quotation, is that the Yogin may have knowledge of all things at once.

Vācaspati says that this citta being essentially of the nature of ahaṃkāra is as all-pervading as the ego itself (IV. 10).

This kāraṇacitta contracts or expands and appears as our individual cittas in our various bodies at successive rebirths. The kāraṇacitta is always connected with the purusha and appears contracted when the purusha presides over animal bodies, and as relatively expanded when he presides over human bodies, and more expanded when he presides over the bodies of gods, etc. This contracted or expanded citta appears as our kāryyacitta which always manifests itself as our states of consciousness. After death the kāraṇacitta, which is always connected with the purusha, manifests itself in the new body which is formed by the āpūra (filling in of prakṛti on account of effective merit or demerit that the purusha had apparently acquired). The formation of the body as well as the contraction or expansion of the kāraṇacitta as the corresponding kāryyacitta to suit it is due to this āpūra. The Yoga does not hold that the citta has got a separate fine astral body within which it may remain encased and be transferred along with it to another body on rebirth. The citta being all-pervading, it appears both to contract or expand to suit the particular body destined for it owing to its merit or demerit, but there is no separate astral body (*Tattvavaiśāradī*, IV. 10). In reality the karaṇacitta as such always remains vibhu or all pervading; it is only its kāryyacitta or vṛtti that appears in a contracted or expanded form, according to the particular body which it may be said to occupy.

The Sāṃkhya view, however, does not regard the citta to be essentially all-pervading, but small or great according as the body it has to occupy. Thus Bhikshu and Nāgeśa in explaining the *Bhāshya,* " others think that the citta expands or contracts according as it is in a bigger or smaller body, just as light rays do according as they are placed in the jug or in a room," attributes this view to the Sāṃkhya (*Vyāsa-bhāshya,* IV. 10, and the commentaries by Bhikshu and Nāgeśa on it).*

It is this citta which appears as the particular states of consciousness in which both the knower and the known are reflected, and it comprehends them both in one state of consciousness. It must, however, be remembered that this citta is essentially a modification of prakṛti, and as such is non-intelligent ; but by the seeming reflection of the purusha it appears as the knower knowing a certain object, and we therefore see that in the states themselves are comprehended both the knower and the known. This citta is not, however, a separate tattva, but is the sum or unity of the eleven senses and the ego and also of the five prāṇas or biomotor forces (*Nāgeśa,* IV. 10). It thus stands for all that is psychical in man : his states of consciousness including the living principle in man represented by the activity of the five prāṇas.

It is the object of Yoga gradually to restrain the citta from its various states and thus cause it to turn back to its original cause, the kāraṇacitta, which is all-pervading. The modifications of the karāṇacitta into such states as the kāryacitta is due to its being overcome by its inherent tamas and rajas ; so when the transformations of the citta into the passing states are arrested by concentration, there takes

* If this is a Sāṃkhya doctrine, it seems clearly to be a case of Jaina influence.

place a backward movement and the all-pervading state of the citta being restored to itself and all tamas being overcome, the Yogin acquires omniscience, and finally when this citta becomes as pure as the form of purusha itself, the purusha becomes conscious of himself and is liberated from the bonds of prakṛti.

The Yoga philosophy in the first chapter describes the Yoga for him whose mind is inclined towards trance-cognition. In the second chapter is described the means by which one with an ordinary worldly mind (*vyutthāna citta*) may also acquire Yoga. In the third chapter are described those phenomena which strengthen the faith of the Yogin on the means of attaining Yoga described in the second chapter. In the fourth chapter is described kaivalya, absolute independence or oneness, which is the end of all the Yoga practices.

The *Bhāshya* describes the five classes of cittas and comments upon their fitness for the Yoga leading to kaivalya. Those are I. *kshipta* (wandering), II. *mūḍha* (forgetful), III. *vikshipta* (occasionally steady), IV. *ekāgra* (one-pointed), *niruddha* (restrained).

I. The *kshiptacitta* is characterised as wandering, because it is being always moved by the rajas. This is that citta which is always moved to and fro by the rise of passions, the excess of which may indeed for the time overpower the mind and thus generate a temporary concentration, but it has nothing to do with the contemplative concentration required for attaining absolute independence. The man moved by rajas, far from attaining any mastery of himself, is rather a slave to his own passions and is always being moved to and fro and shaken by them (see *Siddhānta-candrikā*, I. 2, *Bhojavṛtti*, I. 2).

II. The mūḍhacitta is that which is overpowered by tamas, or passions, like that of anger, etc., by which it loses its senses and always chooses the wrong course. Svāmin

Hariharāraṇya suggests a beautiful example of such concentration as similar to that of certain snakes which become completely absorbed in the prey upon which they are about to pounce.

III. The vikshiptacitta, or distracted or occasionally steady citta, is that mind which rationally avoids the painful actions and chooses the pleasurable ones. Now none of these three kinds of mind can hope to attain that contemplative concentration called Yoga. This last type of mind represents ordinary people, who sometimes tend towards good but relapse back to evil.

IV. The one-pointed (ekāgra) is that kind of mind in which true knowledge of the nature of reality is present and the afflictions due to nescience or false knowledge are thus attenuated and the mind better adapted to attain the nirodha or restrained state. All these come under the saṃprajñāta (concentration on an object of knowledge) type.

V. The nirodha or restrained mind is that in which all mental states are arrested. This leads to kaivalya.

Ordinarily our minds are engaged only in perception, inference, etc.—those mental states which we all naturally possess. These ordinary mental states are full of rajas and tamas. When these are arrested, the mind flows with an abundance of sattva in the saṃprajñāta samādhi; lastly when even the saṃprajñāta state is arrested, all possible states become arrested.

Another important fact which must be noted is the relation of the actual states of mind called the vṛttis with the latent states called the saṃskāras—the potency. When a particular mental state passes away into another, it is not altogether lost, but is preserved in the mind in a latent form as a saṃskāra, which is always trying to manifest itself in actuality. The vṛttis or actual states are thus both generating the saṃskāras and are also always tending to manifest themselves and actually generating similar vṛttis or actual states. There is a circulation from vṛttis to saṃskāras and from them again to vṛttis (*saṃskārāḥ vṛttibhiḥ kriyante, saṃskāraiśca vṛttayaḥ evaṃ vṛttisaṃskāracakramaniśamāvarttate*). So the formation of saṃskāras and their conservation are gradually being strengthened by the habit of similar vṛttis or actual states, and their continuity is again guaranteed by the strength and continuity of these saṃskāras. The saṃskāras are like roots striking deep into the soil and growing with the growth of the plant above, but even when the plant above the soil is destroyed, the roots remain undisturbed and may again shoot forth as plants whenever they obtain a favourable season. Thus it is not enough for a Yogin to arrest any particular class of mental states; he must attain such a habit of restraint that the saṃskāra thus generated is able to overcome, weaken and destroy the saṃskāra of those actual states which he has arrested by his contemplation. Unless restrained by such a habit, the saṃskāra of cessation (*nirodhaja saṃskāra*) which is opposed to the previously acquired mental states become powerful and destroy the latter, these are sure to shoot forth again in favourable season into their corresponding actual states.

The conception of avidyā or nescience is here not negative but has a definite positive aspect. It means that kind of knowledge which is opposed to true knowledge (*vidyāviparītaṃ jñānāntaramavidyā*). This is of four kinds: (1) The thinking of the non-eternal world, which is merely an effect, as eternal. (2) The thinking of the impure as the pure, as for example the attraction that a woman's body may have for a man leading him to think the impure body pure. (3) The thinking of vice as virtue, of the undesirable as the desirable, of pain as pleasure. We know that for a Yogin every phenomenal state of existence is painful (II. 15). A Yogin knows that attachment (*rāga*) to sensual and other objects can only give temporary pleasure, for it is sure to be soon turned into pain. Enjoyment can never bring satisfaction, but only involves a man further and further in sorrows. (4) Considering the non-self, e.g. the body as the self. This causes a feeling of being injured on the injury of the body.

At the moment of enjoyment there is always present suffering from pain in the form of aversion to pain; for the tendency to aversion from pain can only result from the incipient memory of previous sufferings. Of course this is also a case of pleasure turned into pain (*pariṇāmaduḥkhatā*), but it differs from it in this that in the case of pariṇāmaduḥkha pleasure is turned into pain as a result of change or pariṇāma in the future, whereas in this case the anxiety as to pain is a thing of the present, happening at one and the same time that a man is enjoying pleasure.

Enjoyment of pleasure or suffering from pain causes those impressions called saṃskāra or potencies, and these again when aided by association naturally create their memory and thence comes attachment or aversion, then again action, and again pleasure and pain and hence impressions, memory, attachment or aversion, and again action and so forth.

All states are modifications of the three guṇas; in each one of them the functions of all the three guṇas are seen, contrary to one another. These contraries are observable in their developed forms, for the guṇas are seen to abide in various proportions and compose all our mental states. Thus a Yogin who wishes to be released from pain once for all is very sensitive and anxious to avoid even our so-called pleasures. The wise are like the eye-ball. As a thread of wool thrown into the eye pains by merely touching it, but not when it comes into contact with any other organ, so the Yogin is as tender as the eye-ball, when others are insensible of pain. Ordinary persons, however, who have again and again suffered pains as the consequence of their own karma, and who again seek them after having given them up, are all round pierced through as it were by nescience, their minds become full of afflictions, variegated by the eternal residua of the passions. They follow in the wake of the "I" and the "Mine" in relation to things that should be left apart, pursuing threefold pain in repeated births, due to external and internal causes. The Yogin seeing himself and the world of living beings surrounded by the eternal flow of pain, turns for refuge to right knowledge, cause of the destruction of all pains (*Vyāsa-bhāshya*, II. 15).

Thinking of the mind and body and the objects of the external world as the true self and feeling affected by their change is avidyā (false knowledge).

The modifications that this avidyā suffers may be summarised under four heads.

I. The ego, which, as described above, springs from the identification of the buddhi with the purusha.

II. From this ego springs attachment (*rāga*) which is the inclination towards pleasure and consequently towards the means necessary for attaining it in a person who has previously experienced pleasures and remembers them.

II. Repulsion from pain also springs from the ego and is of the nature of anxiety for its removal; anger at pain and the means which produces pain, remains in the mind in consequence of the feeling of pain, in the case of him who has felt and remembers pain.

IV. Love of life also springs from the ego. This feeling exists in all persons and appears in a positive aspect in the form "would that I were never to cease." This is due to the painful experience of death in some previous existence, which abides in us as a residual potency (*vāsanā*) and causes the instincts of self-preservation, fear of death and love of life. These modifications including avidyā are called the five kleśas or afflictions.

We are now in a position to see the far-reaching effects of the identification of the purusha with the buddhi. We have already seen how it has generated the macrocosm or external world on the one hand, and manas and the senses on the other. Now we see that from it also spring attachment to pleasure, aversion from pain and love of life, motives observable in most of our states of consciousness, which are therefore called the *klishṭa vṛtti* or afflicted states. The five afflictions (false knowledge and its four modifications spoken above) just mentioned are all comprehended in avidyā, since avidyā or false knowledge is at the root of all worldly experiences. The sphere of avidyā is all false knowledge generally, and that of asmitā is also inseparably connected with all our experiences which consist in the identification of the intelligent self with the sensual objects of the world, the attainment of which seems to please us and the loss of which is so painful to us. It must, however, be remembered that these five afflictions are only different aspects of avidyā and cannot be conceived separately from avidyā. These always lead us into the meshes of the world, far from our final goal—the realisation of our own self—emancipation of the purusha.

Opposed to it are the vṛttis or states which are called unafflicted, aklishṭa, the habit of steadiness (*abhyāsa*) and non-attachment to pleasures (*vairāgya*) which being antagonistic to the afflicted states, are helpful towards achieving true knowledge. These represent such thoughts as tend towards emancipation and are produced from our attempts to conceive rationally our final state of emancipation, or to adopt suitable means for this. They must not, however, be confused with puṇyakarma (virtuous action), for both puṇya and pāpa karma are said to have sprung from the kleśas. There is no hard and fast rule with regard to the appearance of these klishṭa and aklishṭa states, so that in the stream of the klishṭa states or in the intervals thereof, aklishṭa states may also appear—as practice and desirelessness born from the study of the Veda-reasoning and precepts—and remain quite distinct in itself, unmixed with the klishṭa states. A Brahman being in a village which is full of the Kirātas, does not himself become a Kirāta (a forest tribe) for that reason.

Each aklishṭa state produces its own potency or saṃskāra, and with the frequency of the states their saṃskāra is strengthened which in due course suppresses the aklishṭa states.

These klishṭa and aklishṭa modifications are of five descriptions: pramāṇa (real cognition), viparyyaya (unreal cognition), vikalpa (logical abstraction and imagination), nidrā (sleep), smṛti (memory). These vṛttis or states, however, must be distinguished from the six kinds of mental activity mentioned in *Vyāsa-bhāshya*, II. 18: grahaṇa (reception or presentative ideation), dhāraṇa (retention), ūha (assimilation), apoha (differentiation), tattvajñāna (right knowledge), abhiniveśa (decision and determination), of which these states are the products.

We have seen that from avidyā spring all the kleśas or afflictions, which are therefore seen to be the source of the klishṭa vṛttis as well. Abhyāsa and vairāgya—the aklishṭa vṛttis, which spring from precepts, etc., lead to right knowledge, and as such are antagonistic to the modification of the guṇas on the avidyā side.

We know also that both these sets of vṛttis—the klishṭa and the aklishta—produce their own kinds of saṃskāras, the klishṭa saṃskāra and the aklishṭa or prajñā saṃskāra. All these modifications of citta as vṛtti and saṃskāra are the dharmas of citta, considered as the dharmin or substance.

CHAPTER IX

THE THEORY OF KARMA

THE vṛttis are called the mānasa karmas (mental work) as different from the bāhya karmas (external work) achieved in the exterior world by the five motor or active senses. These may be divided into four classes: (1) kṛshṇa (black), (2) śukla (white), (3) śuklakṛshṇa (white and black), (4) aśuklākṛshṇa (neither white nor black). (1) The kṛshṇa karmas are those committed by the wicked and, as such, are wicked actions called also adharma (demerit). These are of two kinds, viz. bāhya and mānasa, the former being of the nature of speaking ill of others, stealing others' property, etc., and the latter of the nature of such states as are opposed to śraddhā, vīrya, etc., which are called the śukla karma. (2) The śukla karmas are virtuous or meritorious deeds. These can only occur in the form of mental states, and as such can take place only in the mānasa karma. These are śraddhā (faith), vīrya (strength), smṛti (meditation), samādhi (absorption), and prajñā (wisdom), which are infinitely superior to actions achieved in the external world by the motor or active senses. The śukla karma belongs to those who resort to study and meditation. (3) The śuklakṛshṇa karma are the actions achieved in the external world by the motor or active senses. These are called white and black, because actions achieved in the external world, however good (śukla) they might be, cannot be altogether devoid of wickedness (kṛshṇa), since all external actions entail some harm to other living beings.

Even the Vedic duties, though meritorious, are associated with sins, for they entail the sacrificing of animals.*

The white side of these actions, viz.: that of helping others and doing good is therefore called dharma, as it is the cause of the enjoyment of pleasure and happiness for the doer. The kṛshṇa or black side of these actions, viz. that of doing injury to others is called adharma, as it is the cause of the suffering of pain to the doer. In all our ordinary states of existence we are always under the influence of dharma and adharma, which are therefore called vehicles of actions (*āśerate sāṃsārikā purushā asmin niti āśayaḥ*). That in which some thing lives is its vehicle. Here the purushas in evolution are to be understood as living in the sheath of actions (which is for that reason called a vehicle or āśaya). Merit or virtue, and sin or demerit are the vehicles of actions. All śukla karma, therefore, either mental or external, is called merit or virtue and is productive of happiness; all kṛshṇa karma, either mental or external, is called demerit, sin or vice and is productive of pain.

(4) The karma called aśuklakṛshṇa (neither black nor white) is of those who have renounced everything, whose afflictions have been destroyed and whose present body is the last one they will have. Those who have renounced actions, the karma-sannyāsis (and not those who belong to the sannyāsāśrama merely), are nowhere found performing actions which depend upon external means. They have not got the black vehicle of actions, because they do not perform such actions. Nor do they possess the white vehicle of actions, because they dedicate to Īśvara the fruits of all vehicles of action, brought about by the practice of Yoga.

Returning to the question of karmāśaya again for review,

* Compare Pañcaśikha, *svalpasaṇkaraḥ saparihāraḥ sapratyavamarshaḥ, Tattvakaumudī*, 2.

we see that being produced from desire (*kāma*), avarice (*lobha*), ignorance (*moha*), and anger (*krodha*) it has really got at its root the kleśas (afflictions) such as avidyā (ignorance), asmitā (egoism), rāga (attachment), dvesha (antipathy), abhiniveśa (love of life). It will be easily seen that the passions named above, desire, lust, etc., are not in any way different from the kleśas or afflictions previously mentioned ; and as all actions, virtuous or sinful, have their springs in the said sentiments of desire, anger, covetousness, and infatuation, it is quite enough that all these virtuous or sinful actions spring from the the kleśas.

Now this karmāśaya ripens into life-state, life-experience and life-time, if the roots—the afflictions—exist. Not only is it true that when the afflictions are rooted out, no karmāśaya can accumulate, but even when many karmāśayas of many lives are accumulated, they are rooted out when the afflictions are destroyed. Otherwise, it is difficult to conceive that the karmāśaya accumulated for an infinite number of years, whose time of ripeness is uncertain, will be rooted out ! So even if there be no fresh karmāśaya after the rise of true knowledge, the purusha cannot be liberated but will be required to suffer an endless cycle of births and rebirths to exhaust the already accumulated karmāśayas of endless lives. For this reason, the mental plane becomes a field for the production of the fruits of action only, when it is watered by the stream of afflictions. Hence the afflictions help the vehicle of actions (karmāśaya) in the production of their fruits also. It is for this reason that when the afflictions are destroyed the power which helps to bring about the manifestation also disappears ; and on that account the vehicles of actions although existing in innumerable quantities have no time for their fruition and do not possess the power of producing fruit, because their seed-powers are destroyed by intellection.

Karmāśaya is of two kinds (1) Ripening in the same life *dṛshṭajanmavedanīya.* (2) Ripening in another unknown life. That puṇya karmāśaya, which is generated by intense purificatory action, trance and repetition of mantras, and that pāpa karmāśaya, which is generated by repeated evil done either to men who are suffering the extreme misery of fear, disease and helplessness, or to those who place confidence in them or to those who are high-minded and perform tapas, ripen into fruit in the very same life, whereas other kinds of karmāśayas ripen in some unknown life.

Living beings in hell have no dṛshṭajanma karmāśaya, for this life is intended for suffering only and their bodies are called the bhoga-śarīras intended for suffering alone and not for the accumulation of any karmāśaya which could take effect in that very life.

There are others whose afflictions have been spent and exhausted and thus they have no such karmāśaya, the effect of which they will have to reap in some other life. They are thus said to have no adṛshṭa-janmavedanīya karma.

The karmāśaya of both kinds described above ripens into life-state, life-time and life-experience. These are called the three ripenings or vipākas of the karmāśaya ; and they are conducive to pleasure or pain, according as they are products of puṇyakarmāśaya (virtue) or pāpa karmāśaya (vice or demerit). Many karmāśayas combine to produce one life-state; for it is not possible that each karma should produce one or many life-states, for then there would be no possibility of experiencing the effects of the karmas, because if for each one of the karmas we had one or more lives, karmas, being endless, space for obtaining lives in which to experience effects would not be available, for it would take endless time to exhaust the karmas already accumulated. It is therefore held that many karmas unite to produce one life-state or birth (jāti) and to determine also its particular duration (āyush) and experience (bhoga). The virtuous and sinful karmāśayas accumulated in one life, in order to produce their effects, cause the death of the individual and manifest themselves in producing his rebirth, his duration of life and particular experiences, pleasurable or painful. The order of undergoing the experiences is the order in which the karmas manifest themselves as effects, the principal ones being manifested earlier in life. The principal karmas here refer to those which are quite ready to generate their effects. Thus it is said that those karmas which produce their effects immediately are called primary, whereas those which produce effects after some delay are called secondary. Thus we see that there is continuity of existence throughout; when the karmas of this life ripen jointly they tend to fructify by causing another birth as a means to which death is caused, and along with it life is manifested in another body (according to the dharma and adharma of the karmāśaya) formed by the prakṛtyāpūra (cf. the citta theory described above); and the same karmāśaya regulates the life-period and experiences of that life, the karmāśayas of which again take a similar course and manifest themselves in the production of another life and so on.

We have seen that the karmāśaya has three fructifications, viz. jāti, āyush and bhoga. Now generally the karmāśaya is regarded as ekabhavika or unigenital, i.e. it accumulates in one life. Ekabhava means one life and ekabhavika means the product of one life, or accumulated in one life. Regarded from this point of view, it may be contrasted with the vāsanās which remain accumulated from thousands of previous lives since eternity, the mind, being pervaded all over with them, as a fishing-net is covered all over with knots. This vāsanā results from memory of the experiences of a life generated by the fructification of the karmāśaya and kept in the citta in the form of potency or impressions (saṃskāra). Now we have previously seen that the citta remains constant in all the births and rebirths that an individual has undergone from eternity; it therefore keeps the memory of those various experiences of thousands of lives in the form of saṃskāra or potency and is therefore compared with a fishing-net pervaded all over with knots. The vāsanās therefore are not the results of the accumulation of experiences or their memory in one life but in many lives, and are therefore called anekabhavika as contrasted with the karmāśaya representing virtuous and vicious actions which are accumulated in one life and which produce another life, its experiences and its life-duration as a result of fructification (vipāka). This vāsanā is the cause of the instinctive tendencies, or habits of deriving pleasures and pains peculiar to different animal lives.

Thus the habits of a dog-life and its peculiar modes of taking its experiences and of deriving pleasures and pains are very different in nature from those of a man-life; they must therefore be explained on the basis of an incipient memory in the form of potency, or impressions (saṃskāra) of the experiences that an individual must have undergone in a previous dog-life.

Now when by the fructification of the karmāśaya a dog-life is settled for a person, his corresponding vāsanās of a previous dog-life are at once revived and he begins to take interest in his dog-life in the manner of a dog; the same principle applies to the virtue of individuals as men or as gods (IV. 8).

If there was not this law of vāsanās, then any vāsanā would be revived in any life, and with the manifestation of the vāsanā of animal life a man would take interest in eating grass and derive pleasure from it. Thus Nāgeśa says: "Now if those karmas which produce a man-life should manifest the vāsanās of animal lives, then one might be inclined to eat grass as a man, and it is therefore said that only the vāsanās corresponding to the karmas are revived."

Now as the vāsanās are of the nature of saṃskāras or impressions, they lie ingrained in the citta and nothing can prevent their being revived. The intervention of other births has no effect. For this reason, the vāsanās of a dog-life are at once revived in another dog-life, though between the first dog-life and the second dog-life, the individual may have passed through many other lives, as a man, a bull, etc., though the second dog-life may take place many hundreds of years after the first dog-life and in quite different countries. The difference between saṃskāras, impressions, and smṛti or memory is simply this that the former is the latent state whereas the latter is the manifested state; so we see that the memory and the impressions are identical in nature, so that whenever a saṃskāra is revived, it means nothing but the manifestation of the memory of the same experiences conserved in the saṃskāra in a latent state. Experiences, when they take place, keep their impressions in the mind, though thousands of other experiences, lapse of time, etc., may intervene. They are revived in one moment with the proper cause of their revival, and the other intervening experiences can in no way hinder this revival. So it is with the vāsanās, which are revived at once according to the particular fructification of the karmāśaya, in the form of a particular life, as a man, a dog, or anything else.

It is now clear that the karmāśaya tending towards fructification is the cause of the manifestation of the vāsanās already existing in the mind in a latent form. Thus the Sūtra says:—"When two similar lives are separated by many births, long lapses of time and remoteness of space, even then for the purpose of the revival of the vāsanās, they may be regarded as immediately following each other, for the memories and impressions are the same" (*Yoga-sūtra*, IV. 9). The *Bhāshya* says: "the vāsanā is like the memory (smṛti), and so there can be memory from the impressions of past lives separated by many lives and by remote tracts of country. From these memories the impressions (saṃskāras) are derived, and the memories are revived by manifestation of the karmāśayas, and though memories from past impressions may have many lives intervening, these interventions do not destroy the causal antecedence of those past lives " (IV. 9).

These vāsanās are, however, beginningless, for a baby just after birth is seen to feel the fear of death instinctively, and it could not have derived it from its experience in this life. Again, if a small baby is thrown upwards, it is seen to shake and cry like a grown-up man, and from this it may be inferred that it is afraid of falling down on the ground and is therefore shaking through fear. Now this baby has never learnt in this life from experience that a fall on the ground will cause pain, for it has never fallen on the ground and suffered pain therefrom; so the cause of this fear cannot be sought in the experiences of this life, but in the memory of past experiences of fall and pain arising therefrom, which is innate in this life as vāsanā and causes this instinctive fear. So this innate memory which causes instinctive fear of death from the very time of birth, has not its origin in this life but is the memory of the experience of some previous life, and in that life, too, it existed as innate memory of some other previous life, and in that again as the innate memory of some other life and so on to beginningless time. This goes to show that the vāsanās are without beginning.

We come now to the question of unigenitality—ekabhavikatva—of the karmāśaya and its exceptions. We find that great confusion has occurred among the commentators about the following passage in the *Bhāshya* which refers to this subject: The *Bhāshya* according to Vācaspati in II. 13 reads: *tatra dṛshṭajanmavedanīyasya niyatavipākasya*, etc. Here Bhikshu and Nāgeśa read *tatrādṛshṭajanmavedanīyasya niyatavipākasya*, etc. There is thus a divergence of meaning on this point between *Yoga-vārttika* and his follower Nāgeśa, on one side, and Vācaspati on the other.

Vācaspati says that the dṛshṭajanmavedanīya (to be fructified in the same visible life) karma is the only true karma where the karmāśaya is ekabhavika, unigenital, for here these effects are positively not due to the karma of any other previous lives, but to the karma of that very life. Thus these are the only true causes of ekabhavika karmāśaya.

Thus according to Vācaspati we see that the adṛshṭajanmavedanīya karma (to be fructified in another life) of unappointed fruition is never an ideal of ekabhavikatva or unigenital character ; for it may have three different courses : (1) It may be destroyed without fruition. (2) It may become merged in the ruling action. (3) It may exist for a long time overpowered by the ruling action whose fruition has been appointed.

Vijñāna Bhikshu and his follower Nāgeśa, however, say that the dṛshṭajanmavedanīya karma (to be fructified in the same visible life) can never be ekabhavika or unigenital for there is no bhava, or previous birth there, whose product is being fructified in that life, for this karma is of that same visible life and not of some other previous bhava or life ; and they agree in holding that it is for that reason that the *Bhāshya* makes no mention of this dṛshṭajanmavedanīya karma ; it is clear that the karmāśaya in no other bhava is being fructified here. Thus we see that about dṛshṭajanmavedanīya karma, Vācaspati holds that it is the typical case of ekabhavika karma (karma of the same birth), whereas Vijñāna Bhikshu holds just the opposite view, viz. that the dṛhṭajanmavedanīya karma should by no means be considered as ekabhavika since there is here no bhava or birth, it being fructified in the same life.

The adṛshṭajanmavedanīya karma (works to be fructified

in another life) of unfixed fruition has three different courses: (I) As we have observed before, by the rise of *aśuklākṛshṇa* (neither black nor white) karma, the other karmas—*śukla* (black), *kṛshṇa* (white) and *śuklakṛshṇa* (both black and white)—are rooted out. The śukla karmāśaya again arising from study and asceticism destroys the kṛshṇa karmas without their being able to generate their effects. These therefore can never be styled ekabhavika, since they are destroyed without producing any effect. (II) When the effects of minor actions are merged in the effects of the major and ruling action. The sins originating from the sacrifice of animals at a holy sacrifice are sure to produce bad effects, though they may be minor and small in comparison with the good effects arising from the performance of the sacrifice in which they are merged. Thus it is said that the experts being immersed in floods of happiness brought about by their sacrifices bear gladly particles of the fire of sorrow brought about by the sin of killing animals at sacrifice. So we see that here also the minor actions having been performed with the major do not produce their effects independently, and so all their effects are not fully manifested, and hence these secondary karmāśayas cannot be regarded as ekabhavika. (III) Again the adṛshṭajanmavedanīya karma (to be fructified in another life) of unfixed fruition (*aniyata vipāka*) remains overcome for a long time by another adṛshṭajanmavedanīya karma of fixed fruition. A man may for example do some good actions and some extremely vicious ones, so that at the time of death, the karmāśaya of those vicious actions becoming ripe and fit for appointed fruition, generates an animal life. His good action, whose benefits are such as may be reaped only in a man-life, will remain overcome until the man is born again as a man: so this also cannot be said to be ekabhavika (to be reaped in one life). We may summarise the classification of karmas according to Vācaspati in a table as follows:—

Karmāśaya

- Ekabhavika
  - Niyata Vipāka (of fixed fruition).
    - Dṛshṭajanma-vedanīya
    - Adṛshṭajanma-vedanīya
- Anekabhavika
  - Aniyatavipāka
    - Adṛshṭajanmavedanīya
      - (Destruction)
      - (Merged in the effect of the major action.)
      - (To remain overcome by the influence of some other action.)

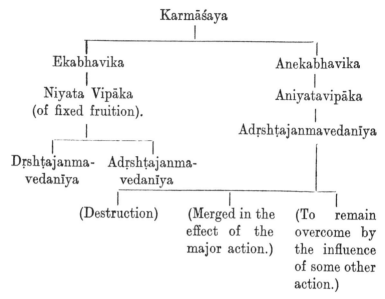

Thus the karmāśaya may be viewed from two sides, one being that of fixed fruition and the other unfixed fruition, and the other that of dṛshṭajanmavedanīya and adṛshṭajanma-vedanīya. Now the theory is that the niyatavipāka (of fixed fruition) karmāśaya is always ekabhavika, i.e. it does not remain separated by other lives, but directly produces its effects in the succeeding life.

Ekabhavika means that which is produced from the accumulation of karmas in one life in the life which succeeds it. Vācaspati, however, takes it also to mean that action which attains fruition in the same life in which it is performed, whereas what Vijñāna Bhikshu understands by ekabhavika is that action alone which is produced in the life immediately succeeding the life in which it was accumulated. So according to Vijñāna Bhikshu, the niyata vipāka (of fixed fruition) dṛshṭajanmavedanīya (to be fructified in the same life) action is not ekabhavika, since it has no bhava, i.e. it is not the production of a preceding life. Neither can it be anekabhavika; thus this niyatavipākadṛshṭajanmavedanīya action is neither ekabhavika nor anekbhavika. Whereas Vācaspati is inclined to call this also ekabhavika. About the niyatavipāka-adṛshṭa-janmavedanīya action being called ekabhavika (unigenital) there seems to be no dispute. The aniyatavipāka-adṛshṭajanmavedanīya action cannot be called ekabhavika as it undergoes three different courses described above.

CHAPTER X

THE ETHICAL PROBLEM

WE have described avidyā and its special forms as the kleśas, from which also proceed the actions virtuous and vicious, which in their turn again produce as a result of their fruition, birth, life and experiences of pleasure and pain and the vāsanās or residues of the memory of these experiences. Again every new life or birth is produced from the fructification of actions of a previous life; a man is made to perform actions good or bad by the kleśas which are rooted in him, and these actions, as a result of their fructification, produce another life and its experiences, in which life again new actions are earned by virtue of the kleśas, and thus the cycle is continued. When there is pralaya or involution of the cosmical world-process the individual cittas of the separate purushas return back to the prakṛti and lie within it, together with their own avidyās, and at the time of each new creation or evolution these are created anew with such changes as are due according to their individual avidyās, with which they had to return back to their original cause, the prakṛti, and spend an indivisible inseparable existence with it. The avidyās of some other creation, being merged in the prakṛti along with the cittas, remain in the prakṛti as vāsanās, and prakṛti being under the influence of these avidyās as vāsanās creates as modifications of itself the corresponding minds for the individual purushas, connected with them before the last pralaya dissolution. So we see that though the cittas had returned to their original causes with their individual nescience (*avidyā*), the avidyā was not lost but was revived at the time of the new creation and created such minds as should be suitable receptacles for it. These minds (buddhi) are found to be modified further into their specific cittas or mental planes by the same avidyā which is manifested in them as the kleśas, and these again in the karmāśaya, jāti, āyush and bhoga, and so on; the individual, however, is just in the same position as he was or would have been before the involution of pralaya. The avidyās of the cittas which had returned to the prakṛti at the time of the creation being revived, create their own buddhis of the previous creation, and by their connection with the individual purushas are the causes of the saṃsāra or cosmic evolution—the evolution of the microcosm, the cittas, and the macrocosm or the exterior world.

In this new creation, the creative agencies of God and avidyā are thus distinguished in that the latter represents the end or purpose of the prakṛti—the ever-evolving energy transforming itself into its modifications as the mental and the material world; whereas the former represents that intelligent power which abides outside the pale of prakṛti, but removes obstructions offered by the prakṛti. Though unintelligent and not knowing how and where to yield so as to form the actual modifications necessary for the realisation of the particular and specific objects of the numberless purushas, these avidyās hold within themselves the serviceability of the purushas, and are the cause of the connection of the purusha and the prakṛti, so that when these avidyās are rooted out it is said that the purushārthatā or serviceability of the purusha is at an end and the purusha becomes liberated from the bonds of prakṛti, and this is called the final goal of the purusha.

The ethical problem of the Pātañjala philosophy is the uprooting of this avidyā by the attainment of true knowledge of the nature of the purusha, which will be succeeded by the liberation of the purusha and his absolute freedom or independence—kaivalya—the last realisation of the purusha—the ultimate goal of all the movements of the prakṛti.

This final uprooting of the avidyā with its vāsanās directly follows the attainment of true knowledge called prajñā, in which state the seed of false knowledge is altogether burnt and cannot be revived again. Before this state, the discriminative knowledge which arises as the recognition of the distinct natures of purusha and buddhi remains shaky; but when by continual practice this discriminative knowledge becomes strengthened in the mind, its potency gradually grows stronger and stronger, and roots out the potency of the ordinary states of mental activity, and thus the seed of false knowledge becomes burnt up and incapable of fruition, and the impurity of the energy of rajas being removed, the sattva as the manifesting entity becomes of the highest purity, and in that state flows on the stream of the notion of discrimination—the recognition of the distinct natures of purusha and buddhi—free from impurity. Thus when the state of buddhi becomes almost as pure as the purusha itself, all self-enquiry subsides, the vision of the real form of the purusha arises, and false knowledge, together with the kleśas and the consequent fruition of actions, ceases once for all. This is that state of citta which, far from tending towards the objective world, tends towards the kaivalya of the purusha.

In the first stages, when the mind attains discriminative knowledge, the prajñā is not deeply seated, and occasionally phenomenal states of consciousness are seen to intervene in the form of "I am," "Mine," "I know," "I do not know," because the old potencies, though becoming weaker and weaker are not finally destroyed, and consequently occasionally produce their corresponding conscious manifestation as states which impede the flow of discriminative knowledge.

But constant practice in rooting out the potency of this state destroys the potencies of the outgoing activity, and finally no intervention occurs in the flow of the stream of prajñā through the destructive influence of phenomenal states of consciousness. In this higher state when the mind is in its natural, passive, and objectless stream of flowing prajñā, it is called the dharmamegha-samādhi. When nothing is desired even from dhyāna arises the true knowledge which distinguishes prakṛti from purusha and is called the dharmamegha-samādhi (*Yoga-sūtra*, IV. 29). The potency, however, of this state of consciousness lasts until the purusha is finally liberated from the bonds of prakṛti and is absolutely free (kevalī). Now this is the state when the citta becomes infinite, and all its tamas being finally overcome, it shines forth like the sun, which can reflect all, and in comparison to which the crippled insignificant light of objective knowledge shrinks altogether, and thus an infinitude is acquired, which has absorbed within itself all finitude, which cannot have any separate existence or manifestation through this infinite knowledge. All finite states of knowledge are only a limitation of true infinite knowledge, in which there is no limitation of this and that. It absorbs within itself all these limitations.

The purusha in this state may be called the emancipated being, jīvanmukta. Nāgeśa in explaining *Vyāsa-bhāshya*, IV. 31, describing the emancipated life says: "In this jīvanmukta stage, being freed from all impure afflictions and karmas, the consciousness shines in its infirmity. The infiniteness of consciousness is different from the infiniteness of materiality veiled by tamas. In those stages there could be consciousness only with reference to certain things with reference to which the veil of tamas was raised by rajas. When all veils and impurities are removed, then little is left which is not known. If there were other categories besides the 25 categories, these also would then have been known" (*Chāyāvyākhyā*, IV. 31).

Now with the rise of such dharmamegha the succession of the changes of the qualities is over, inasmuch as they have fulfilled their object by having achieved experience and emancipation, and their succession having ended, they cannot stay even for a moment. And now comes absolute freedom, when the guṇas return back to the pradhāna their primal cause, after performing their service for the purusha by providing his experience and his salvation, so that they lose all their hold on purusha and purusha remains as he is in himself, and never again has any connection with the buddhi. The purusha remains always in himself in absolute freedom.

The order of the return of the guṇas for a kevalī purusha is described below in the words of Vācaspati: The guṇas as cause and effect involving ordinary experiences samādhi and nirodha, become submerged in the manas; the manas becomes submerged in the asmitā, the asmitā in the liṅga, and the liṅga in the aliṅga.

This state of kaivalya must be distinguished from the state of mahāpralaya in which also the guṇas return back to prakṛti, for that state is again succeeded by later connections of prakṛti with purushas through the buddhis, but the state of kaivalya is an eternal state which is never again disturbed by any connection with prakṛti, for now the separation of prakṛti from purusha is eternal, whereas that in the mahāpralaya state was only temporary.

We shall conclude this section by noting two kinds of eternity of purusha and of prakṛti, and by offering a criticism of the prajñā state. The former is said to be perfectly and unchangeably eternal (*kūṭastha nitya*), and the latter is only eternal in an evolutionary form. The permanent or eternal reality is that which remains unchanged amid its changing appearances; and from this point of view both purusha and prakṛti are eternal. It is indeed true, as we have seen just now, that the succession of changes of qualities with regard to buddhi, etc., comes to an end when kaivalya is attained, but this is with reference to purusha, for the changes of qualities in the guṇas themselves never come to an end. So the guṇas in themselves are eternal in their changing or evolutionary character, and are therefore said to possess evolutionary eternity (*pariṇāminityatā*). Our phenomenal conception cannot be free from change, and therefore it is that in our conception of the released purushas we affirm their existence, as for example when we say that the released purushas exist eternally. But it must be carefully noted that this is due to the limited character of our thoughts and expressions, not to the real nature of the released purushas, which remain for ever unqualified by any changes or modifications, pure and colourless as the very self of shining intelligence (see *Vyāsa-bhāshya*, IV. 33).

We shall conclude this section by giving a short analysis of the prajñā state from its first appearance to the final release of purusha from the bondage of prakṛti. Patañjali says that this prajñā state being final in each stage is sevenfold. Of these the first four stages are due to our conscious endeavour, and when these conscious states of prajñā (supernatural wisdom) flow in a stream and are not hindered or interfered with in any way by other phenomenal coscinous states of pratyayas the purusha becomes finally liberated through the natural backward movement of the citta to its own primal cause, and this backward movement is represented by the other three stages.

The seven prajñā stages may be thus enumerated:—

I. The pain to be removed is known. Nothing further remains to be known of it.

This is the first aspect of the prajñā, in which the person

willing to be released knows that he has exhausted all that is knowable of the pains.

II. The cause of the pains has been removed and nothing further remains to be removed of it. This is the second stage or aspect of the rise of prajñā.

III. The nature of the extinction of pain has already been perceived by me in the state of samādhi, so that I have come to learn that the final extinction of my pain will be something like it.

IV. The final discrimination of prakṛti and purusha, the true and immediate means of the extinction of pain, has been realised.

After this stage, nothing remains to be done by the purusha himself. For this is the attainment of final true knowledge. It is also called the para vairāgya. It is the highest consummation, in which the purusha has no further duties to perform. This is therefore called the kārya vimukti (or salvation depending on the endeavour of the purusha) or jīvanmukti.

After this follows the citta vimukti or the process of release of the purusha from the citta, in three stages.

V. The aspect of the buddhi, which has finally finished its services to purusha by providing scope for purusha's experiences and release; so that it has nothing else to perform for purusha. This is the first stage of the retirement of the citta.

VI. As soon as this state is attained, like the falling of stones thrown from the summit of a hill, the guṇas cannot remain even for a moment to bind the purusha, but at once return back to their primal cause, the prakṛti; for the avidyā being rooted out, there is no tie or bond which can keep it connected with purusha and make it suffer changes for the service of purusha. All the purushārthatā being ended, the guṇas disappear of themselves.

VII. The seventh and last aspect of the guṇas is that they never return back to bind purusha again, their teleological purpose being fulfilled or realised. It is of course easy to see that, in these last three stages, purusha has nothing to do ; but the guṇas of their own nature suffer these backward modifications and return back to their own primal cause and leave the purusha kevalī (for ever solitary). *Vyāsa-bhāshya*, II. 15.

Vyāsa says that as the science of medicine has four divisions : (1) disease, (2) the cause of disease, (3) recovery, (4) medicines ; so this Yoga philosophy has also four divisions, viz. : (I) Saṃsāra (the evolution of the prakṛti in connection with the purusha). (II) The cause of saṃsāra. (III) Release. (IV) The means of release.

Of these the first three have been described at some length above. We now direct our attention to the fourth. We have shown above that the ethical goal, the ideal to be realised, is absolute freedom or kaivalya, and we shall now consider the line of action that must be adopted to attain this goal—the *summum bonum.* All actions which tend towards the approximate realisation of this goal for man are called kuśala, and the man who achieves this goal is called kuśalī. It is in the inherent purpose of prakṛti that man should undergo pains which include all phenomenal experiences of pleasures as well, and ultimately adopt such a course of conduct as to avoid them altogether and finally achieve the true goal, the realisation of which will extinguish all pains for him for ever. The motive therefore which prompts a person towards this ethico-metaphysical goal is the avoidance of pain. An ordinary man feels pain only in actual pain, but a Yogin who is as highly sensitive as the eye-ball, feels pain in pleasure as well, and therefore is determined to avoid all experiences, painful or so-called pleasurable. The extinguishing of all experiences, however, is not the true ethical goal, being only a means to the realisation of kaivalya or the true self and nature of the purusha. But this means represents the highest end of a person, the goal beyond which all his duties cease; for after this comes kaivalya which naturally manifests itself on the necessary retirement of the prakṛti. Purusha has nothing to do in effectuating this state, which comes of itself. The duties of the purusha cease with the thorough extinguishing of all his experiences. This therefore is the means of extinguishing all his pains, which are the highest end of all his duties; but the complete extinguishing of all pains is identical with the extinguishing of all experiences, the states or vṛttis of consciousness, and this again is identical with the rise of prajñā or true discriminative knowledge of the difference in nature of prakṛti and its effects from the purusha—the unchangeable. These three sides are only the three aspects of the same state which immediately precede kaivalya. The prajñā aspect is the aspect of the highest knowledge, the suppression of the states of consciousness or experiences, and it is the aspect of the cessation of all conscious activity and of painlessness or the extinguishing of all pains as the feeling aspect of the same nirvīja—samādhi state. But when the student directs his attention to this goal in his ordinary states of experience, he looks at it from the side of the feeling aspect, viz. that of acquiring a state of painlessness, and as a means thereto he tries to purify the mind and be moral in all his actions, and begins to restrain and suppress his mental states, in order to acquire this nirvīja or seedless state. This is the sphere of conduct which is called Yogāṅga.

Of course there is a division of duties according to the advancement of the individual, as we shall have occasion to show hereafter. This suppression of mental states which has been described as the means of attaining final release, the ultimate ethical goal of life, is called Yoga. We have said before that of the five kinds of mind—kshipta, mūḍha, vikshipta, ekāgra, niruddha—only the last two are fit for the process of Yoga and ultimately acquire absolute freedom. In the other three, though concentration may occasionally happen, yet there is no extrication of the mind from the afflictions of avidyā and consequently there is no final release.

CHAPTER XI

YOGA PRACTICE

THE Yoga which, after weakening the hold of the afflictions and causing the real truth to dawn upon our mental vision, gradually leads us towards the attainment of our final goal, is only possible for the last two kinds of minds and is of two kinds: (1) samprajñāta (cognitive) and (2) asamprajñāta (ultra-cognitive). The samprajñāta Yoga is that in which the mind is concentrated upon some object, external or internal, in such a way that it does not oscillate or move from one object to another, but remains fixed and settled in the object that it holds before itself. At first, the Yogin holds a gross material object before his view, but when he can make himself steady in doing this, he tries with the subtle tanmātras, the five causes of the grosser elements, and when he is successful in this he takes his internal senses as his object and last of all, when he has fully succeeded in these attempts, he takes the great egohood as his object, in which stage his object gradually loses all its determinate character and he is said to be in a state of suppression in himself, although devoid of any object. This state, like the other previous states of the samprajñāta type, is a positive state of the mind and not a mere state of vacuity of objects or negativity. In this state, all determinate character of the states disappears and their potencies only remain alive. In the first stages of a Yogin practising samādhi conscious states of the lower stages often intervene, but gradually, as the mind becomes fixed, the potencies of the lower stages are overcome by the potencies of this stage, so that the mind flows in a calm current and at last the higher prajñā dawns, whereupon the potencies of this state also are burnt and extinguished, the citta returns back to its own primal cause, prakṛti, and purusha attains absolute freedom.

The first four stages of the samprajñāta state are called *madhumatī*, *madhupratīka*, *viśoka* and the *saṃskāraśesha* and also *vitarkānugata*, *vicārānugata*, *ānandānugata* and *asmitānugata*. True knowledge begins to dawn from the first stage of this samprajñāta state, and when the Yogin reaches the last stage the knowledge reaches its culminating point, but still so long as the potencies of the lower stages of relative knowledge remain, the knowledge cannot obtain absolute certainty and permanency, as it will always be threatened with a possible encroachment by the other states of the past phenomenal activity now existing as the subconscious. But the last stage of asamprajñāta samādhi represents the stage in which the ordinary consciousness has been altogether surpassed and the mind is in its own true infinite aspect, and the potencies of the stages in which the mind was full of finite knowledge are also burnt, so that with the return of the citta to its primal cause, final emancipation is effected. The last state of samprajñāta samādhi is called saṃskāraśesha, only because here the residua of the potencies of subconscious thought only remain and the actual states of consciousness become all extinct. It is now easy to see that no mind which is not in the ekāgra or one-pointed state can be fit for the asamprajñāta samādhi in which it has to settle itself on one object and that alone. So also no mind which has not risen to the state of highest suppression is fit for the asamprajñāta or nirvīja state.

It is now necessary to come down to a lower level and examine the obstructions, on account of which a mind cannot easily become one-pointed or ekāgra. These, nine in number, are the following:—

Disease, languor, indecision, want of the mental requirements necessary for samādhi, idleness of body and mind, attachment to objects of sense, false and illusory knowledge, non-attainment of the state of concentrated contemplation, unsteadiness and unstability of the mind in a samādhi state even if it can somehow attain it. These are again seen to be accompanied with pain and despair owing to the non-fulfilment of desire, physical shakiness or unsteadiness of the limbs, taking in of breath and giving out of it, which are seen to follow the nine distractions of a distracted mind described above.

To prevent these distractions and their accompaniments it is necessary that we should practise concentration on one truth. Vācaspati says that this one truth on which the mind should be settled and fixed is Īśvara, and Rāmānanda Sarasvatī and Nārāyaṇa Tīrtha agree with him. Vijñāna Bhikshu, however, says that one truth means any object, gross or fine, and Bhoja supports Vijñāna Bhikshu, saying that here "one truth" might mean any desirable object.

Abhyāsa means the steadiness of the mind in one state and not complete absence of any state; for the Bhāshyakāra himself has said in the samāpattisūtra, that samprajñāta trance comes after this steadiness. As we shall see later, it means nothing but the application of the five means, śraddhā, vīrya, smṛti, samādhi and prajñā; it is an endeavour to settle the mind on one state, and as such does not differ from the application of the five means of Yoga with a view to settle and steady the mind (*Yoga-vārttika*, I. 13). This effort becomes firmly rooted, being well attended to for a long time without interruption and with devotion.

Now it does not matter very much whether this one truth is Īśvara or any other object; for the true principle of Yoga is the setting of the mind on one truth, principle or object. But for an ordinary man this is no easy matter; for in order to be successful the mind must be equipped with śraddhā or faith—the firm conviction of the Yogin in the course that he adopts. This keeps the mind steady, pleased, calm and free from doubts of any kind, so that the Yogin may proceed to the realisation of his object without any vacillation. Unless a man has a firm hold on the course that he pursues, all the steadiness that he may acquire will constantly be threatened with the danger of a sudden collapse. It will be seen that vairāgya or desirelessness is only the negative aspect of this śraddhā. For by it the mind is restrained from the objects of sense, with an aversion or dislike towards the objects of sensual pleasure and worldly desires; this aversion towards worldly joys is only the other aspect of the faith of the mind and the calmness of its currents (*cittaprasāda*) towards right knowledge and absolute freedom. So it is said that the vairāgya is the effect of śraddhā and its product (*Yoga-vārttika*, I. 20). In order to make a person suitable for Yoga, vairāgya represents the cessation of the mind from the objects of sense and their so-called pleasures, and śraddhā means the positive faith of the mind in the path of Yoga that one adopts, and the right aspiration towards attaining the highest goal of absolute freedom.

In its negative aspect, vairāgya is of two kinds, apara and para. The apara is that of a mind free from attachment to worldly enjoyments, such as women, food, drinks and power, as also from thirst for heavenly pleasures attainable by practising the vedic rituals and sacrifices. Those who are actuated by apara vairāgya do not desire to remain in a bodiless state (*videha*) merged in the senses or merged in the prakṛti (*prakṛtilīna*). It is a state in which the mind is indifferent to all kinds of pleasures and pains. This vairāgya may be said to have four stages: (1) Yatamāna—in which sensual objects are discovered to be defective and the mind recoils from them. (2) Vyatireka—in which the senses to be conquered are noted. (3) Ekendriya—in which attachment towards internal pleasures and aversion towards external pains, being removed, the mind sets before it the task of removing attachment and aversion towards mental passions for obtaining honour or avoiding dishonour, etc. (4) The fourth and last stage of vairāgya called vaśīkāra is that in which the mind has perceived the futility of all attractions towards external objects of sense and towards the pleasures of heaven, and having suppressed them altogether feels no attachment, even should it come into connection with them.

With the consummation of this last stage of apara vairāgya, comes the para vairāgya which is identical with the rise of the final prajñā leading to absolute independence. This vairāgya, śraddhā and the abhyāsa represent the unafflicted states (aklishṭavṛtti) which suppress gradually the klishṭa or afflicted mental states. These lead the Yogin from one stage to another, and thus he proceeds higher and higher until the final state is attained.

As vairāgya advances, śraddha also advances; from śraddhā comes vīrya, energy, or power of concentration (*dhāraṇā*); and from it again springs smṛti—or continuity of one object of thought; and from it comes samādhi or cognitive and ultra-cognitive trance; after which follows prajñā, cognitive and ultra-cognitive trance; after which follows prajñā and final release. Thus by the inclusion of śraddhā within vairāgya, its effect, and the other products of śraddhā with abhyāsa, we see that the abhyāsa and vairāgya are the two internal means for achieving the final goal of the Yogin, the supreme suppression and extinction of all states of consciousness, of all afflictions and the avidyā—the last state of supreme knowledge or prajñā.

As śraddhā, vīrya, smṛti, samādhi which are not different

from vairāgya and abhyāsa (they being only their other aspects or simultaneous products), are the means of attaining Yoga, it is possible to make a classification of the Yogins according to the strength of these with each, and the strength of the quickness (*saṃvega*) with which they may be applied towards attaining the goal of the Yogin. Thus Yogins are of nine kinds :—

(1) mildly energetic, (2) of medium energy, (3) of intense energy.

Each of these may vary in a threefold way according to the mildness, medium state, or intensity of quickness or readiness with which the Yogin may apply the means of attaining Yoga. There are nine kinds of Yogins. Of these the best is he whose mind is most intensely engaged and whose practice is also the strongest.

There is a difference of opinion here about the meaning of the word saṃvega, between Vācaspati and Vijñāna Bhikshu. The former says that saṃvega means vairāgya here, but the latter holds that saṃvega cannot mean vairāgya, and vairāgya being the effect of śraddhā cannot be taken separately from it. "Saṃvega" means quickness in the performance of the means of attaining Yoga; some say that it means "vairāgya." But that is not true, for if vairāgya is an effect of the due performance of the means of Yoga, there cannot be the separate ninefold classification of Yoga apart from the various degrees of intensity of the means of Yoga practice. Further, the word "saṃvega" does not mean "vairāgya" etymologically (*Yoga-vārttika*, I. 20).

We have just seen that śraddhā, etc., are the means of attaining Yoga, but we have not discussed what purificatory actions an ordinary man must perform in order to attain śraddhā, from which the other requisites are derived. Of course these purificatory actions are not the same for all, since they must necessarily depend upon the conditions of purity or impurity of each mind; thus a person already in an advanced state, may not need to perform those purificatory actions necessary for a man in a lower state. We have just said that Yogins are of nine kinds, according to the strength of their mental acquirements—śraddhā, etc.—the requisite means of Yoga and the degree of rapidity with which they may be applied. Neglecting division by strength or quickness of application along with these mental requirements, we may again divide Yogins again into three kinds: (1) Those who have the best mental equipment. (2) Those who are mediocres. (3) Those who have low mental equipment.

In the first chapter of Yoga aphorisms, it has been stated that abhyāsa, the application of the mental acquirements of śraddhā, etc., and vairāgya, the consequent cessation of the mind from objects of distraction, lead to the extinction of all our mental states and to final release. When a man is well developed, he may rest content with his mental actions alone, in his abhyāsa and vairāgya, in his dhāraṇā (concentration), dhyāna (meditation), and samādhi (trance), which may be called the jñānayoga. But it is easy to see that this jñānayoga requires very high mental powers and thus is not within easy reach of ordinary persons. Ordinary persons whose minds are full of impurities, must pass through a certain course of purificatory actions before they can hope to obtain those mental acquirements by which they can hope to follow the course of jñānayoga with facility.

These actions, which remove the impurities of the mind, and thus gradually increase the lustre of knowledge, until the final state of supreme knowledge is acquired, are called kriyāyoga. They are also called yogāṅgas, as they help the maturity of the Yoga process by gradually increasing the lustre of knowledge. They represent the means by which even an ordinary mind (*vikshiptacitta*) may gradually purify itself and become fit for the highest ideals of Yoga. Thus the

Bhāshya says : " By the sustained practice of these yogāṅgas or accessories of Yoga is destroyed the fivefold unreal cognition (*avidyā*), which is of the nature of impurity. Destruction means here disappearance ; thus when that is destroyed, real knowledge is manifested. As the means of achievement are practised more and more, so is the impurity more and more attenuated. And as more and more of it is destroyed, so does the light of wisdom go on increasing more and more. This process reaches its culmination in discriminative knowledge, which is knowledge of the nature of purusha and the guṇas.

CHAPTER XII

THE YOGĀṄGAS

Now the assertion that these actions are the causes of the attainment of salvation brings up the question of the exact natures of their operation with regard to this supreme attainment. Bhāshyakara says with respect to this that they are the causes of the separation of the impurities of the mind just as an axe is the cause of the splitting of a piece of wood; and again they are the causes of the attainment of the supreme knowledge just as dharma is the cause of happiness. It must be remembered that according to the Yoga theory causation is viewed as mere transformation of energy; the operation of concomitant causes only removes obstacles impeding the progress of these transformations in a particular direction; no cause can of itself produce any effect, and the only way in which it can help the production of an effect into which the causal state passes out of its own immanent energy by the principles of conservation and transformation of energy, is by removing the intervening obstacles. Thus just as the passage of citta into a happy state is helped by dharma removing the intervening obstacles, so also the passage of the citta into the state of attainment of true knowledge is helped by the removal of obstructions due to the performance of the yogāṅgas; the necessary obstructions being removed, the citta passes naturally of itself into this infinite state of attainment of true knowledge, in which all finitude is merged.

In connection with this, Vyāsa mentions nine kinds of operation of causes: (1) cause of birth; (2) of preservation; (3) of manifestation; (4) of modification; (5) knowledge of a premise leading to a deduction; (6) of otherness; (7) of separation; (8) of attainment; (9) of upholding (*Vyāsa-bhāshya*, II. 28.)

The principle of conservation of energy and transformation of energy being the root idea of causation in this system, these different aspects represent the different points of view in which the word causation is generally used.

Thus, the first aspect as the cause of birth or production is seen when knowledge springs from manas which renders indefinite cognition definite so that mind is called the cause of the birth of knowledge. Here mind is the material cause (*upādāna kāraṇa*) of the production of knowledge, for knowledge is nothing but manas with its particular modifications as states (*Yoga-vārttika*, II. 18). The difference of these positive cause from *āptikāraṇa*, which operates only in a negative way and helps production, in an indirect way by the removal of obstacles, is quite manifest. The *sthitikāraṇa* or cause through which things are preserved as they are, is the end they serve; thus the serviceability of purusha is the cause of the existence and preservation of the mind as it is, and not only of mind but of all our phenomenal experiences.

The third cause of the *abhivyaktikāraṇa* or manifestation which is compared to a lamp which manifests things before our view is an epistemological cause, and as such includes all sense activity in connection with material objects which produce cognition.

Then come the fourth and the fifth causes, vikāra (change) and pratyaya (inseparable connection); thus the cause of change (*vikāra*) is exemplified as that which causes a change; thus the manas suffers a change by the objects presented to it, just as bile changes and digests the food that is eaten; the cause of pratyaya* is that in which from inseparable connection, with the knowledge of the premise (e.g. there is smoke in the hill) we can also have inferential knowledge of the other (e.g. there is fire in the hill). The sixth cause as otherness (*anyatva*) is that which effects changes of form as that brought about by a goldsmith in gold when he makes a bangle from it, and then again a necklace, is regarded as differing from the change spoken of as vikāra. Now the difference between the gold being turned into bangles or necklaces and the raw rice being turned into soft rice is this, that in the former case when bangles are made out of gold, the gold remains the same in each case, whereas in the case of the production of cooked rice from raw by fire, the case is different, for heat changes paddy in a far more definite way; goldsmith and heat are both indeed efficient causes, but the former only effects mechanical changes of shape and form, whereas the latter is the cause of structural and chemical changes. Of course these are only examples from the physical world, their causal operations in the mental sphere varying in a corresponding manner; thus the change produced in the mind by the presentation of different objects, follows a law which is the same as is found in the physical world, when the same object causes different kinds of feelings in different persons; when ignorance causes forgetfulness in a thing, anger makes it painful and desire makes it pleasurable, but knowledge of its true reality produces indifference; there is thus the same kind of causal change as is found in the external world. Next for consideration is the cause of separation (*viyoga*) which is only a negative aspect of the positive side of the causes of transformations, as in the gradual extinction of impurities, consequent upon the transformation of the citta towards the attainment of the supreme state of absolute independence

* Pratyaya is explained in *Yoga-vārttika*, II. 28, as *sampratyaya* or *prāmāṇyaniścaya*.

through discriminative knowledge. The last cause for consideration is that of upholding (*dhṛti*) ; thus the body upholds the senses and supports them for the actualisation of their activities in the body, just as the five gross elements are the upholding causes of organic bodies ; the bodies of animals, men, etc., also employ one another for mutual support. Thus the human body lives by eating the bodies of many animals ; the bodies of tigers, etc., live on the bodies of men and other animals ; many animals live on the bodies of plants, etc. (*Tattvavaiśāradī*, II. 28). The four kinds of causes mentioned in Śaṅkara's works and grammatical commentaries like that of Susheṇa, viz. : utpādya, vikāryya, āpya and saṃskāryya, are all included within the nine causes contained mentioned by Vyāsa.

The yogāṅgas not only remove the impurities of the mind but help it further by removing obstacles in the way of attaining the highest perfection of discriminative knowledge. Thus they are the causes in a double sense (1) of the dissociation of impurities (*viyogakāraṇa*) ; (2) of removing obstacles which impede the course of the mind in attaining the highest development (*āptikāraṇa*).

Coming now to the yogāṅgas, we enumerate them thus :—restraint, observance, posture, regulation of breath, abstraction, concentration, meditation and trance : these are the eight accessories of Yoga.

It must be remembered that abhyāsa and vairāgya and also the five means of attaining Yoga, viz. : śraddhā, vīryya, etc., which are not different from abhyāsa and vairāgya, are by their very nature included within the yogāṅgas mentioned above, and are not to be considered as independent means different from them. The parikarmas or embellishments of the mind spoken of in the first chapter, with which we shall deal later on, are also included under the three yogāṅgas dhāraṇā, dhyāna and samādhi. The five means śraddhā, vīryya, smṛti, samādhi and prajñā are said to be included under asceticism (*tapaḥ*) studies (*svādhyāya*) and devotion to God of the niyamas and vairāgya in contentment.

In order to understand these better, we will first give the definitions of the yogāṅgas and then discuss them and ascertain their relative values for a man striving to attain the highest perfection of Yoga.

I. Yama (restraint). These yama restraints are: abstinence from injury (ahiṃsā); veracity; abstinence from theft; continence; abstinence from avarice.

II. Niyama (observances). These observances are cleanliness, contentment, purificatory action, study and the making of God the motive of all action.

III. Āsanas (posture). Steady posture and easy position are regarded as an aid to breath control.

IV. Regulation of breath (prāṇāyāma) is the stoppage of the inspiratory and expiratory movements (of breath) which may be practised when steadiness of posture has been secured.

V. Pratyāhāra (abstraction). With the control of the mind all the senses become controlled and the senses imitate as it were the vacant state of the mind. Abstraction is that by which the senses do not come in contact with their objects and follow as it were the nature of the mind.

VI. Dhāraṇā (concentration). Concentration is the steadfastness of the mind applied to a particular object.

VII. Dhyāna (mediation). The continuation there of the mental effort by continually repeating the object is meditation (dhyāna).

VIII. Samādhi (trance contemplation). The same as above when shining with the light of the object alone, and devoid as it were of itself, is trance. In this state the mind becomes one with its object and there is no difference between the knower and the known.

These are the eight yogāṅgas which a Yogin must adopt for

his higher realisation. Of these again we see that some have the mental side more predominant, while others are mostly to be actualised in exterior action. Dhāraṇā, dhyāna and samādhi, which are purely of the samprajñāta type, and also the prāṇāyāma and pratyāhāra, which are accessories to them, serve to cleanse the mind of impurities and make it steady, and can therefore be assimilated with the parikarmas mentioned in Book I. Sūtras 34–39. These samādhis of the samprajñāta type, of course, only serve to steady the mind and to assist attaining discriminative knowledge.

In this connection, it will be well to mention the remaining aids for cleansing the mind as mentioned in *Yoga-sūtra* I., viz. the cultivation of the habits of friendliness, compassion, complacency and indifference towards happiness, misery, virtue and vice.

This means that we are to cultivate the habit of friendliness towards those who are happy, which will remove all jealous feelings and purify the mind. We must cultivate the habit of compassion towards those who are suffering pain; when the mind shows compassion (which means that it wishes to remove the miseries of others as if they were his own) it becomes cleansed of the stain of desire to do injury to others, for compassion is only another name for sympathy which naturally identifies the compassionate one with the objects of his sympathy. Next comes the habit of complacency, which one should diligently cultivate, for it leads to pleasure in virtuous deeds. This removes the stain of envy from the mind. Next comes the habit of indifference, which we should acquire towards vice in vicious persons. We should acquire the habit of remaining indifferent where we cannot sympathise; we should not on any account get angry with the wicked or with those with whom sympathy is not possible. This will remove the stain of anger. It will be clearly seen here that maītrī, karuṇā, muditā and upekshā are only different aspects of universal sympathy, which should remove all perversities in our nature and unite us with our fellow-beings. This is the positive aspect of the mind with reference to abstinence from injuring ahiṃsā (mentioned under yamas), which will cleanse the mind and make it fit for the application of means of śraddhā, etc. For unless the mind is pure, there is no scope for the application of the means of making it steady. These are the mental endeavours to cleanse the mind and to make it fit for the proper manifestation of śraddhā, etc., and for steadying it with a view to attaining true discriminative knowledge.

Again of the parikarmas by dhāraṇā, dhyāna, and saṃprajñāta samādhi and the habit of sympathy as manifested in maitrī, karuṇā, etc., the former is a more advanced state of the extinction of impurities than the latter.

But it is easy to see that ordinary minds can never commence with these practices. They are naturally so impure that the positive universal sympathy as manifested in maitrī, etc., by which turbidity of mind is removed, is too difficult. It is also difficult for them to keep the mind steady on an object as in dhāranā, dhyāna, and samādhi, for only those in advanced stages can succeed in this. For ordinary people, therefore, some course of conduct must be discovered by which they can purify their minds and elevate them to such an extent that they may be in a position to avail themselves of the mental parikarmas or purifications just mentioned. Our minds become steady in proportion as their impurities are cleansed. The cleansing of impurities only represents the negative aspect of the positive side of making the mind steady. The grosser impurities being removed, finer ones remain, and these are removed by the mental parikarmas, supplemented by abhyāsa or by śraddhā, etc. As the impurities are gradually more and more attenuated, the last germs of impurity are destroyed by the force of dhyāna or the habit of nirodha samādhi, and kaivalya is attained.

We now deal with yamas, by which the gross impurities of ordinary minds are removed. They are, as we have said before, non-injury, truthfulness, non-stealing, continence, and non-covetousness ; of these non-injury is given such a high place that it is regarded as the root of the other yamas ; truthfulness, non-stealing, continence, non-covetousness and the other niyamas mentioned previously only serve to make the non-injury perfect. We have seen before that maitrī, karuṇa, muditā and upekshā serve to strengthen the non-injury since they are only its positive aspects, but we see now that not only they but other yamas and also the other niyamas, purity, contentment, asceticism, studies and devotion to God, only serve to make non-injury more and more perfect. This non-injury when it is performed without being limited or restricted in any way by caste, country, time and circumstances, and is always adhered to, is called mahāvrata or the great duty of abstinence from injury. It is sometimes limited to castes, as for example injury inflicted by a fisherman, and in this case it is called anuvrata or restricted ahiṃsā of ordinary men as opposed to universal ahiṃsā of the Yogins called mahāvrata ; the same non-injury is limited by locality, as in the case of a man who says to himself, " I shall not cause injury at a sacred place " ; or by time, when a person says to himself, " I shall not cause injury on the sacred day of Caturdaśī " ; or by circumstances, as when a man says to himself, " I shall cause injury for the sake of gods and Brahmans only " ; or when injury is caused by warriors in the battle-field alone and nowhere else. This restricted ahiṃsā is only for ordinary men who cannot follow the Yogin's universal law of ahiṃsā.

Ahiṃsā is a great universal duty which a man should impose on himself in all conditions of life, everywhere, and at all times without restricting or qualifying it with any limitation whatsoever. In *Mahābhārata Mokshadharmādhyāya* it is said that the Sāṃkhya lays stress upon non-injury, whereas the Yoga lays stress upon samādhi; but here we see that Yoga also holds that ahiṃsā should be the greatest ethical motive for all our conduct. It is by ahiṃsā alone that we can make ourselves fit for the higher type of samādhi. All other virtues of truthfulness, non-stealing only serve to make non-injury more and more perfect. It is not, however, easy to say whether the Sāṃkhyists attached so much importance to non-injury that they believed it to lead to samādhi directly without the intermediate stages of samādhi. We see, however, that the Yoga also attaches great importance to it and holds that a man should refrain from all external acts; for however good they may be they cannot be such as not to lead to some kind of injury or hiṃsā towards beings, for external actions can never be performed without doing some harm to others. We have seen that from this point of view Yoga holds that the only pure works (śuklakarma) are those mental works of good thoughts in which perfection of ahiṃsā is attained. With the growth of good works (śuklakarma) and the perfect realisation of non-injury the mind naturally passes into the state in which its actions are neither good (śukla) nor bad (aśukla); and this state is immediately followed by that of kaivalya.

Veracity consists in word and thought being in accordance with facts. Speech and mind correspond to what has been seen, heard and inferred. Speech is for the purpose of transferring knowledge to another. It is always to be employed for the good of others and not for their injury; for it should not be defective as in the case of Yudhishṭhira, where his motive was bad.* If it prove to be injurious to living beings,

* Yudhishṭhira led falsely Droṇa to believe that the latter's son was dead by inaudibly muttering that it was only an elephant having the same name as that of his son that had died.

even though uttered as truth, it is not truth ; it is sin only. Though outwardly such a truthful course may be considered virtuous, yet since by his truth he has caused injury to another person, he has in reality violated the true standard of non-injury (*ahiṃsā*). Therefore let everyone first examine well and then utter truth for the benefit of all living beings. All truths should be tested by the canon of non-injury (*ahiṃsā*).

Asteya is the virtue of abstaining from stealing. Theft is making one's own unlawfully things that belong to others. Abstinence from theft consists in the absence of the desire thereof.

Brahmacaryya (continence) is the restraint of the generative organ and the thorough control of sexual tendencies.

Aparigraha is want of avariciousness, the non-appropriation of things not one's own ; this is attained on seeing the defects of attachment and of the injury caused by the obtaining, preservation and destruction of objects of sense.

If, in performing the great duty of non-injury and the other virtues auxiliary to it, a man be troubled by thoughts of sin, he should try to remove sinful ideas by habituating himself to those which are contrary to them. Thus if the old habit of sins opposed to virtues tend to drive him along the wrong path, he should in order to banish them entertain ideas such as the following :—" Being burnt up as I am in the fires of the world, I have taken refuge in the practice of Yoga which gives protection to all living beings. Were I to resume the sins which I have abandoned, I should certainly be behaving like a dog, which eats its own vomit. As the dog takes up his own vomit, so should I be acting if I were to take up again what I have once given up." This is called the practice of *pratipaksha bhāvān*, meditating on the opposites of the temptations.

A classification of sins of non-injury, etc., may be made according as they are actually done, or caused to be done, or permitted to be done ; and these again may be further divided according as they are preceded by desire, anger or ignorance; these are again mild, middling or intense. Thus we see that there may be twenty-seven kinds of such sins. Mild, middling and intense are each again threefold, mild-mild, mild-middling and mild-intense; middling-mild, middling-middling and middling-intense; also intense-mild, intense-middling and intense-intense. Thus there are eighty-one kinds of sins. But they become infinite on account of rules of restriction, option and conjunction.

The contrary tendency consists in the notion that these immoral tendencies cause an infinity of pains and untrue knowledge. Pain and unwisdom are the unending fruits of these immoral tendencies, and in this idea lies the power which produces the habit of giving a contrary trend to our thoughts.

These yamas, together with the niyamas about to be described, are called kriyāyoga, by the performance of which men become fit to rise gradually to the state of jñānayoga by samādhi and to attain kaivalya. This course thus represents the first stage with which ordinary people should begin their Yoga work.

Those more advanced, who naturally possess the virtues mentioned in Yama, have no need of beginning here.

Thus it is said that some may begin with the niyamas, asceticism, svādhyāya and devotion to God; it is for this reason that, though mentioned under the niyamas, they are also specially selected and spoken of as the kriyāyoga in the very first rule of the second Book. Asceticism means the strength of remaining unchanged in changes like that of heat and cold, hunger and thirst, standing and sitting, absence of speech and absence of all indications by gesture, etc.

Svādhyāya means the study of philosophy and repetition of the syllable "Aum."

This Īśvarapraṇidhāna (devotion to God) is different from the Īśvarapraṇidhāna mentioned in *Yoga-sūtra*, I. 23, where it meant love, homage and adoration of God, by virtue of which God by His grace makes samādhi easy for the Yogin.

Here it is a kind of kriyāyoga, and hence it means the bestowal of all our actions upon the Great Teacher, God, i.e. to work, not for one's own self but for God, so that a man desists from all desires for fruit therefrom.

When these are duly performed, the afflictions become gradually attenuated and trance is brought about. The afflictions thus attenuated become characterised by unproductiveness, and when their seed-power has, as it were, been burnt up by the fire of high intellection and the mind untouched by afflictions realises the distinct natures of purusha and sattva, it naturally returns to its own primal cause prakṛti and kaivalya is attained.

Those who are already far advanced do not require even this kriyāyoga, as their afflictions are already in an attenuated state and their minds in a fit condition to adapt themselves to samādhi ; they can therefore begin at once with jñānayoga. So in the first chapter it is with respect to these advanced men that it is said that kaivalya can be attained by abhyāsa and vairāgya, without adopting the kriyāyoga (*Yoga-vārttika*, II. 2) kriyāyogas. Only śauca and santosha now remain to be spoken of. Śauca means cleanliness of body and mind. Cleanliness of body is brought about by water, cleanliness of mind by removal of the mental impurities of pride, jealousy and vanity.

Santosha (contentment) is the absence of desire to possess more than is necessary for the preservation of one's life. It should be added that this is the natural result of ceasing to desire to appropriate the property of others.

At the close of this section on the yamas and niyamas, it is best to note their difference, which lies principally in this that the former are the negative virtues, whereas the latter are positive. The former can, and therefore must, be practised at all stages of Yoga, whereas the latter being positive are attainable only by distinct growth of mind through Yoga. The virtues of non-injury, truthfulness, sex-restraint, etc., should be adhered to at all stages of the Yoga practice. They are indispensable for steadying the mind.

It is said that in the presence of a person who has acquired steadiness in ahiṃsā all animals give up their habits of enmity; when a person becomes steady in truthfulness, whatever he says becomes fulfilled. When a person becomes steady in asteya (absence of theft) all jewels from all quarters approach him.

Continence being confirmed, vigour is obtained. Non-covetousness being confirmed, knowledge of the causes of births is attained. By steadiness of cleanliness, disinclination to this body and cessation of desire for other bodies is obtained.

When the mind attains internal śauca, or cleanliness of mind, his sattva becomes pure, and he acquires highmindedness, one-pointedness, control of the senses and fitness for the knowledge of self. By the steadiness of contentment comes the acquisition of extreme happiness. By steadiness of asceticism the impurities of this body are removed, and from that come miraculous powers of endurance of the body and also miraculous powers of the sense, viz. clairaudience and thought-reading from a distance. By steadiness of studies the gods, the ṛshis and the siddhas become visible. When Īśvara is made the motive of all actions, trance is attained. By this the Yogin knows all that he wants to know, just as it is in reality, whether in another place, another body or another time. His intellect knows everything as it is.

It should not, however, be said, says Vācaspati, that inasmuch as the samprajñāta is attained by making Īśvara the motive of all actions, the remaining seven yogāṅgas are useless. For the yogāṅgas are useful in the attainment of that mental mood which devotes all actions to the purposes of

Īśvara. They are also useful in the attainment of saṃprajñāta samādhi by separate kinds of collocations, and samādhi also leads to the fruition of saṃprajñāta, but though this meditation on Īśvara is itself a species of Īśvarapraṇidhāna, samprajñāta Yoga is a yet more direct means. As to the relation of Īśvarapraṇidhāna with the other aṅgas of Yoga, Bhikshu writes :—It cannot be asked what is the use of the other disciplinary practices of the Yoga since Yoga can be attained by meditation on Īśvara, for meditation on Īśvara only removes ignorance. The other accessories bring about samādhi by their own specific modes of operation. Moreover, it is by help of meditation on Īśvara that one succeeds in bringing about samādhi, through the performance of all the accessories of Yoga ; so the accessories of Yoga cannot be regarded as unnecessary ; for it is the accessories which produce dhāraṇā, dhyāna and samādhi, through meditation on God, and thereby salvation ; devotion to God brings in His grace and through it the yogāṅgas can be duly performed. So though devotion to God may be considered as the direct cause, it cannot be denied that the due performance of the yogāṅgas is to be considered as the indirect cause.

Āsanas are secured when the natural involuntary movements cease, and this may be effected by concentrating the mind on the mythological snake which quietly bears the burden of the earth on its head. Thus posture becomes perfect and effort to that end ceases, so that there is no movement of the body ; or the mind is transformed into the infinite, which makes the idea of infinity its own and then brings about the perfection of posture. When posture has once been mastered there is no disturbance through the contraries of heat and cold, etc.

After having secured stability in the Āsanas the prāṇāyāmas should be attempted. The pause that comes after a deep inhalation and that after a deep exhalation are each called a prāṇāyāma ; the first is external, the second internal. There is, however, a third mode, by means of which, since the lungs are neither too much dilated nor too much contracted, total restraint is obtained ; cessation of both these motions takes place by a single effort, just as water thrown on a heated stone shrivels up on all sides.

These can be regulated by calculating the strength of inhalation and exhalation through space, time or number. Thus as the breathing becomes slower, the space that it occupies also becomes smaller and smaller. Space again is of two kinds, internal and external. At the time of inhalation, the breath occupies internal space, which can be felt even in the soles of hand and feet, like the slight touch of an ant. To try to feel this touch along with deep inhalation serves to lengthen the period of cessation of breathing. External space is the distance from the tip of the nose to the remotest point at which breath when inhaled can be felt, by the palm of the hand, or by the movement of any light substance like cotton, etc., placed there. Just as the breathing becomes slower and slower, the distances traversed by it also becomes smaller and smaller. Regulations by time is seen when the attention is fixed upon the time taken up in breathing by moments, a moment (*kshaṇa*) is the fourth part of the twinkling of the eye. Regulation by time thus means the fact of our calculating the strength of the prāṇāyāma the moments or kshaṇas spent in the acts of inspiration, pause and respiration. These prāṇāyāmas can also be measured by the number of moments in the normal duration of breaths. The time taken by the respiration and expiration of a healthy man is the same as that measured by snapping the fingers after turning the hand thrice over the knee and is the measure of duration of normal breath ; the first attempt or udghāta called mild is measured by thirty-six such mātrās or measures ; when doubled it is the second udghāta called middling ; when trebled it is the third udghāta called intense. Gradually the Yogin acquires the practice of prāṇāyāma of long duration, by daily practice increasing in succession from a day, a fortnight, a month, etc. Of course he proceeds first by mastering the first udghāta, then the second, and so on until the duration increases up to a day, a fortnight, a month as stated. There is also a fourth kind of prāṇāyāma transcending all these stages of unsteady practice, when the Yogin is steady in his cessation of breath. It must be remembered, however, that while the prāṇāyāmas are being practised, the mind must be fixed by dhyāna and dhāraṇā to some object external or internal, without which these will be of no avail for the true object of Yoga. By the practice of prāṇāyāma, mind becomes fit for concentration as described in the *sūtra* I. 34, where it is said that steadiness is acquired by prāṇāyāma in the same way as concentration, as we also find in the *sūtra* II. 53.

When the senses are restrained from their external objects by pratyāhāra we have what is called pratyāhāra, by which the mind remains as if in its own nature, being altogether identified with the object of inner concentration or contemplation; and thus when the citta is again suppressed, the senses, which have already ceased coming into contact with other objects and become submerged in the citta, also cease along with it. Dhāraṇā is the concentration of citta on a particular place, which is so very necessary at the time of prāṇāyāmas mentioned before. The mind may thus be held steadfast in such places as the sphere of the navel, the lotus of the heart, the light in the brain, the forepart of the nose, the forepart of the tongue, and such like parts of the body.

Dhyāna is the continuance or changing flow of the mental effort in the object of dhāraṇā unmediated by any other break of conscious states.

Samādhi, or trance-contemplation, results when by deep concentration mind becomes transformed into the shape of the object of contemplation. By pratyāhāra or power of abstraction, mind desists from all other objects, except the one on which it is intended that it should be centred ; the Yogin, as he thus abstracts his mind, should also try to fix it upon some internal or external object, which is called dhāraṇā ; it must also be noticed that to acquire the habit of dhāraṇā and in order to inhibit the abstraction arising from shakiness and unsteadiness of the body, it is necessary to practise steadfast posture and to cultivate the praṇayama. So too for the purpose of inhibiting distractions arising from breathing. Again, before a man can hope to attain steadfastness in these, he must desist from any conduct opposed to the yamas, and also acquire the mental virtues stated in the niyamas, and thus secure himself against any intrusion of distractions arising from his mental passions. These are the indirect and remote conditions which qualify a person for attaining dhāraṇā, dhyāna, and samādhi. A man who through his good deeds or by the grace of God is already so much advanced that he is naturally above all such distractions, for the removal of which it is necessary to practise the yamas, the niyamas, the āsanas, the prāṇāyāma and pratyāhara, may at once begin with dhāraṇā ; dhāraṇā we have seen means concentration, with the advancement of which the mind becomes steady in repeating the object of its concentration, i.e. thinking of that thing alone and no other thing ; thus we see that with the practice of this state called dhyāna, or meditation, in which the mind flows steadily in that one state without any interruption, gradually even the conscious flow of this activity ceases and the mind, transformed into the shape of the object under concentration, becomes steady therein. We see therefore that samādhi is the consummation of that process which begins in dhāraṇā or concentration. These three, dhāraṇā, dhyāna and samādhi, represent the three stages of the same process of which the last one is the perfection ; and these three are together technically called saṃyama, which directly leads to and is immediately followed by the samprajñāta state, whereas the other five yogāṅgas are only its indirect or remote causes. These three are, however, not essential for the asamprajñāta state, for a person who is very far advanced, or one who is the special object of God's grace, may pass at once by intense vairāgya and abhyāsa into the nirodha state or state of suppression.

As the knowledge of samādhi gradually dawns through the possession of saṃyama, so is the saṃyama gradually strengthened. For this saṃyama also rises higher and higher with the dawning of prajñāloka or light of samādhi knowledge. This is the beginning, for here the mind can hold saṃyama or concentrate and become one with a gross object together with its name, etc., which is called the savitarka state; the next plane or stage of saṃyama is that where the mind becomes one with the object of its meditation, without any consciousness of its name, etc. Next come the other two stages called savicāra and nirvicāra when the mind is fixed on subtle substances, as we shall see later on.

CHAPTER XIII

STAGES OF SAMĀDHI

SAṂPRAJÑĀTA samādhi (absorptive concentration in an object) may be divided into four classes, savitarka, nirvitarka, savicāra and nirvicāra.

To comprehend its scope we must first of all understand the relation between a thing, its concept, and the particular name with which the concept or thing is associated. It is easy to see that the thing (*artha*), the concept (*jñāna*), and the name (*śabda*) are quite distinct. But still, by force of association, the word or name stands both for the thing and its concept; the function of mind, by virtue of which despite this unreality or want of their having any real identity of connection they seem to be so much associated that the name cannot be differentiated from the thing or its idea, is called vikalpa.

Now that state of samādhi in which the mind seems to become one with the thing, together with its name and concept, is the lowest stage of samādhi called savitarka; it is the lowest stage, because here the gross object does not appear to the mind in its true reality, but only in the false illusory way in which it appears associated with the concept and the name in ordinary life. This state does not differ from ordinary conceptual states, in which the particular thing is not only associated with the concepts and their names, but also with other concepts and their various relations; thus a cow will not only appear before the mind with its concept and name, but also along with other relations and thoughts associated with cows, as for example—"This is a cow, it belongs to so and so, it has so many hairs on its body, and so forth." This state is therefore the first stage of samādhi, in which the mind has not become steady and is not as yet beyond the range of our ordinary consciousness.

The nirvitarka stage arises from this when the mind by its steadiness can become one with its object, divested of all other associations of name and concept, so that it is in direct touch with the reality of the thing, uncontaminated by associations. The thing in this state does not appear to be an object of my consciousness, but my consciousness becoming divested of all "I" or "mine," becomes one with the object itself; so that there is no such notion here as "I know this," but the mind becomes one with the thing, so that the notion of subject and object drops off and the result is the one steady transformation of the mind into the object of its contemplation. This state brings home to us real knowledge of the thing, divested from other false and illusory associations, which far from explaining the real nature of the object, serves only to hide it. This samādhi knowledge or prajñā is called nirvitarka. The objects of this state may be the gross material objects and the senses.

Now this state is followed by the state of savicārā prajñā, which dawns when the mind neglecting the grossness of the object sinks deeper and deeper into its finer constituents; the appearance of the thing in its grosser aspects drops off and the mind having sunk deep, centres in and identifies itself with the subtle tanmātras, which are the constituents of the atoms, as a conglomeration of which the object appeared before our eyes in the nirvitarka state. Thus when the mind, after identifying itself with the sun in its true aspect as pure light, tends to settle on a still finer state of it, either by making the senses so steady that the outward appearance vanishes, or by seeking finer and finer stages than the grosser manifestation of light as such, it apprehends the tanmātric state of the light and knows it as such, and we have what is called the savicāra stage. It has great similarities with the savitarka stage, while its differences from that stage spring from the fact that here the object is the tanmātra and not the gross bhūta. The mind in this stage holding communion with the rūpa tanmātra, for example, is not coloured variously as red, blue, etc., as in the savitarka communion with gross light, for the tanmātric light or light potential has no such varieties as different kinds of colour, etc., so that there are also no such different kinds of feeling of pleasure or pain as arise from the manifold varieties of ordinary light. This is a state of feelingless representation of one uniform tanmātric state, when the object appears as a conglomeration of tanmātras of rūpa, rasa or gandha, as the case might be. This state, however, is not indeterminate, as the nirvitarka stage, for this tanmātric conception is associated with the notions of time, space and causality, for the mind here feels that it sees those tanmātras which are in such a subtle state that they are not associated with pleasures and pains. They are also endowed with causality in such a way that from them and their particular collocations originate the atoms.

It must be noted here that the subtle objects of concentration in this stage are not the tanmātras alone, but also other subtle substances including the ego, the buddhi and the prakṛti.

But when the mind acquires the complete habit of this state in which it becomes identified with these fine objects—the tanmātras—etc., then all conceptual notions of the associations of time, space, casuality, etc., spoken of in the savicāra and the savitarka state vanish away and it becomes one with the fine object of its communion. These two kinds of prajñā, savicāra and nirvicāra, arising from communion with the fine tanmātras, have been collocated under one name as vicārānugata. But when the object of communion is the senses, the samādhi is called ānandānugata, and when the object of communion is the subtle cause the ego (*asmitā*), the samādhi is known as asmitānugata.

There is a difference of opinion regarding the object of the last two varieties of samādhi, viz. ānandānugata and asmitānugata, and also about the general scheme of division of the samādhis. Vācaspati thinks that *Yoga-sūtra* I. 41 suggests the interpretation that the samprajñāta samādhis may be divided into three different classes according as their objects of concentration belong to one or other of the three different planes of grāhya (external objects), grahaṇa (the senses) and grahītṛ (the ego). So he refers vitarka and vicāra to the plane of grāhya (physical objects and tanmātras), ānandānugata to the plane of grahaṇa (the senses) and asmitānugata to the plane of grahītṛ. Bhikshu, however, disapproves of such an interpretation. He holds that in ānandānugata the object of concentration is bliss (ānanda) and not the senses. When the Yogin rises to the vicārānugata stage there is a great flow of sattva which produces bliss, and at this the mind becomes one with this ānanda or bliss, and this samādhi is therefore called ānandānugata. Bhikshu does not think that in asmitānugata samādhi the object of concentration is the ego. He thinks that in this stage the object of concentration is the concept of self (*kevalapurushākārā saṃvit*) which has only the form of ego or " I " (*asmītyetāvanmātrākāratvādasmitā*).

Again according to Vācaspati in addition to the four varieties of savitarka, nirvitarka, savicāra and nirvicāra there are two varieties of ānandanugata as sānanda and nirānanda and two varieties of asmitānugata as sāsmita and nirasmita. This gives us eight different kinds of samādhi. With Bhikshu there are only six kinds of samādhi, for he admits only one variety as ānandānugata and one variety as asmitānugata. Bhikshu's classification of samādhis is given below in a tabular form (see

Vācaspati's *Tattvavaiśāradī* and *Yoga-vārttika*, I. 17, 41, 42, 43, 44).

- samprajñāta samādhi
  - sthūlavishayaka (vitarkānugata) samādhi
    - 1. savitarka (with associations of name and concept of the object)
    - 2. nirvitarka (without association of name)
  - sūkshma vishayaka
    - tanmātra vicārānugata samādhi
      - 3. savicāra (with association of name and concept of the tanmātras)
      - 4. nirvicāra (without association of name, etc.)
    - ānanda
      - 5. (ānandānugata)
    - asmitā or purusha
      - 6. (asmitānugata)

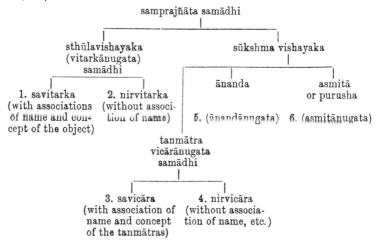

Through the nirvicāra state our minds become altogether purified and there springs the prajñā or knowledge called ṛtambharā or true ; this true knowledge is altogether different from the knowledge which is derived from the Vedas or from inferences or from ordinary perceptions ; for the knowledge that it can give of Reality can never be had by any other means, by perception, inference or testimony, for their communication is only by the conceptual process of generalisations and abstractions and these can never help us to affirm anything about things as they are in themselves, which are altogether different from their illusory demonstrations in conceptual terms which only prevent us from knowing the true reality. The potency of this prajñā arrests the potency of ordinary states of consciousness and thus attains stability. When, however, this prajñā is also suppressed, we have what is called the state of nirvīja samādhi, at the end of which comes final prajñā leading to the dissolution of the citta and the absolute freedom of the purusha.

Samādhi we have seen is the mind's becoming one with an object by a process of acute concentration upon it and a continuous repetition of it with the exclusion of all other thoughts of all kinds. We have indeed described the principal stages of the advancement of samprajñāta Yoga, but it is impossible to give an exact picture of it with the symbolical expressions of our concepts ; for the stages only become clear to the mental vision of the Yogin as he gradually acquires firmness in his practice. The Yogin who is practising at once comes to know them as the higher stages gradually dawn in his mind and he distinguishes them from each other ; it is thus a matter of personal experience, so that no teacher can tell him whether a certain stage which follows is higher or lower, for Yoga itself is its own teacher.

Even when the mind is in the samprajñāta state it is said to be in vyutthāna (phenomenal) in comparison with the nirodha state, just as the ordinary conscious states are called vyutthāna in comparison with the samprajñāta state ; the potencies of the samprajñāta state become weaker and weaker, while the potencies of the nirodha state become stronger and stronger until finally the mind comes to the nirodha state and becomes stable therein ; of course this contains within itself a long mental history, for the potency of the nirodha state can become stronger only when the mind practises it and remains in this suppressed condition for long intervals of time. This shows that the mind, being made up of the three guṇas, is always suffering transformations and changes. Thus from the ordinary state of phenomenal consciousness it gradually becomes one-pointed and then gradually becomes transformed into the state of an object (internal or external), when it is said to be undergoing the samādhi pariṇāma or samādhi change of the samprajñāta type ; next comes the change, when the mind passes from the samprajñāta stage to the state of suppression (*nirodha*). Here also, therefore, we see that the same dharma, lakshṇa, avasthāpariṇāma which we have already described at some length with regard to sensible objects apply also to the mental states. Thus the change from the vyutthāna (ordinary experience) to the nirodha state is the dharmapariṇāma, the change as manifested in time, so that we can say that the change of vyutthāna into nirodha has not yet come, or has just come, or that the vyutthāna state (ordinary experience) exists no longer, the mind having transformed itself into the nirodha state. There is also here the third change of condition, when we see that the potencies of the samprajñāta state become weaker and weaker, while that of the nirodha state becomes stronger and stronger. These are the three kinds of change which the mind undergoes called the dharma, lakshaṇa and avasthā change. But there is one difference between this change thus described from the changes observed in sensible objects that here the changes are not visible but are only to be inferred by the passage of the mind from one state to another.

It has been said that there are two different kinds of qualities of the mind, visible and invisible. The visible qualities whose changes can be noticed are conscious states, or thought-products, or percepts, etc. The invisible ones are seven in number and cannot be directly seen, but their existence and changes or modifications may be established by inference. These are suppression, characterisation, subconscious maintenance of experience, constant change, life, movement and power or energy.

In connection with samprajñāta samādhi some miraculous attainments are described, which are said to strengthen the faith or belief of the Yogin in the processes of Yoga as the path of salvation. These are like the products or the mental experiments in the Yoga method, by which people may become convinced of the method of Yoga as being the true one. No reasons are offered as to the reason for these attainments, but they are said to happen as a result of mental union with different objects. It is best to note them here in a tabular form.

Object of Saṃyama.	Saṃyama.	Attainment.
(1) Threefold change of things as dharma, lakshaṇa and avasthāpariṇāma.	Saṃyama.	
(2) The distinctions of name, external object and the concept which ordinarily appears united as one.	,,	Knowledge of the sounds of all living beings.
(3) Residual potencies saṃskāra of the nature of dharma and adharma.	,,	Knowledge of previous life.
(4) Concepts alone (separated from the objects).	,,	Knowledge of other minds.
(5) Over the form of body.	,,	Disappearance (by virtue of perceptibility being checked).
(6) Karma of fast or slow fruition.	,,	Knowledge of death.
(7) Friendliness, sympathy, and compassion.	,,	Power.
(8) Powers of elephant.	,,	Power of elephant.
(9) Sun.	,,	Knowledge of the world (the geographical position of countries, etc.).
(10) Heavens.	,,	Knowledge of the heavenly systems.
(11) Pole star.	,,	Knowledge of its movements.
(12) Plenus of the navel.	,,	Knowledge of the system of the body.
(13) Base of the throat	,,	Subdual of hunger and thirst.

Object or Saṃyama.	Saṃyama.	Attainment.
(14) Tortoise tube.	Saṃyama.	Steadiness.
(15) Coronal light.	,,	Vision of the perfected ones—the knowledge of the seer, or all knowledge by prescience.
(16) Heat.	,,	Knowledge of the mind.
(17) Purusha.	,,	Knowledge of purusha.
(18) Gross nature subtle pervasiveness and purposefulness.	,,	Control over the element from which follows attenuation, perfection of the body and non-resistance by their characteristics.
(19) Act, substantive appearance, egoism, pervasiveness and purposefulness of sensation.	,,	Mastery over the senses; thence quickness of mind, unaided mental perception and mastery over the pradhāna.

These vibhūtis, as they rise with the performance of the processes of Yoga, gradually deepen the faith *śraddha* of the Yogin in the performance of his deeds and thus help towards his main goal or ideal by always pushing or drawing him forward towards it by the greater and greater strengthening of his faith. Divested from the ideal, they have no value.

CHAPTER XIV

GOD IN YOGA

AFTER describing the nature of karmayoga, and the way in which it leads to jñānayoga, we must now describe the third and easiest means of attaining salvation, the bhaktiyoga and the position of Īśvara in the Yoga system, with reference to a person who seeks deliverance from the bonds and shackles of avidyā.

Īśvara in the Yoga system is that purusha who is distinguished from all others by the fact of his being untouched by the afflictions or the fruits of karma. Other purushas are also in reality untouched by the afflictions, but they, seemingly at least, have to undergo the afflictions and consequently birth and rebirth, etc., until they are again finally released; but Īśvara, though he is a purusha, yet does not suffer in any way any sort of bondage. He is always free and ever the Lord. He never had nor will have any relation to these bonds. He is also the teacher of the ancient teachers beyond the range of conditioning time.

This nature of Īśvara has been affirmed in the scriptures and is therefore taken as true on their authority. The authority of the scriptures is again acknowledged only because they have proceeded from God or Īśvara. The objection that this is an argument in a circle has no place here, since the connection of the scriptures with Īśvara is beginningless.

There is no other divinity equal to Īśvara, because in the case of such equality there might be opposition between rival

Īśvaras, which might result in the lowering in degree of any of them. He is omniscient in the highest degree, for in him is the furthest limit of omniscience, beyond which there is nothing.

This Īśvara is all-merciful, and though he has no desires to satisfy, yet for the sake of his devotees he dictates the Vedas at each evolution of the world after dissolution. But he does not release all persons, because he helps only so far as each deserves; he does not nullify the law of karma, just as a king, though quite free to act in any way he likes, punishes or rewards people as they deserve.

At the end of each kalpa, he adopts pure body from his sattva, which is devoid of any karmāśaya, and thus communicates through it to all his devotees and dictates the Vedas. Again at the time of dissolution this body of pure sattva becomes submerged in prakṛti; and at the time of its submersion, Īśvara wishes that it might come forth again at the beginning of the new creation; thus for ever at each new creation the pure sattva body springs forth and is submerged again into prakṛti at the time of the dissolution of the universe.

In accepting this body he has no personal desires to satisfy, as we have said before. He adopts it only for the purpose of saving mankind by instructing them as to knowledge and piety, which is not possible without a pure sattvamaya body; so he adopts it, but is not affected in any way by it. One who is under the control of nescience cannot distinguish his real nature from nescience, and thus is always led by it, but such is not the case with Īśvara, for he is not in any way under its control, but only adopts it as a means of communicating knowledge to mankind.

A Yogin also who has attained absolute independence may similarly accept one or more pure sattvamaya nirmāṇa cittas from asmitāmātra and may produce one citta as the superintendent of all these. Such a citta adopted by a true Yogin by the force of his meditation is not under the control of the vehicles of action as is the case with the other four kinds of citta from birth, oshadhi, mantra and tapas.

The praṇava or oṃkāra is his name ; though at the time of dissolution, the word of praṇava together with its denotative power becomes submerged in the prakṛti, to reappear with the new creation, just as roots shoot forth from the ground in the rainy season. This praṇava is also called svādhyāya. By concentration of this svādhyāya or praṇava, the mind becomes one-pointed and fit for Yoga.

Now one of the means of attaining Yoga is Īśvarapraṇidhāna, or worship of God. This word, according to the commentators, is used in two senses in the first and the second books of the Pātañjala Yoga aphorisms. In the first book it means love or devotion to God as the one centre of meditation, in the second it is used to mean the abnegation of all desires of the fruits of action to Īśvara, and thus Īśvarapraṇidhāna in this sense is included under kriyāyoga. This dedication of all fruits of action to Īśvara, purifies the mind and makes it fit for Yoga and is distinguished from the Īśvarapraṇidhāna of the first book as the bhāvanā of praṇava and Īśvara in this that it is connected with actions and the abnegation of their fruits, whereas the latter consists only in keeping the mind in a worshipful state towards Īśvara and his word or name praṇava.

By devotion (bhakti) Īśvara is drawn towards the devotee through his nirmāṇa citta of pure sattva and by his grace he removes all obstructions of illness, etc., described in I. 30, 31, and at once prepares his mind for the highest realisation of his own absolute independence. So for a person who can love and adore Īśvara, this is the easiest course of attaining samādhi. We can make our minds pure most easily by abandoning all our actions to Īśvara and attaining salvation by firm and steady devotion to Him. This is the sphere of bhaktiyoga by which the tedious complexity of the Yoga process may be avoided and salvation speedily acquired by the supreme grace of Īśvara.

This means is not, however, distinct from the general means of Yoga, viz. abhyāsa and vairāgya, which applies to all stages. For here also abhyāsa applies to the devotion of Īśvara as one supreme truth and vairāgya is necessarily associated with all true devotion and adoration of Īśvara.

This conception of Īśvara differs from the conception of Īśvara in the Rāmānuja system in this that there prakṛti and purusha, acit and cit, form the body of Īśvara, whereas here Īśvara is considered as being only a special purusha with the aforesaid powers.

In this system Īśvara is not the superintendent of prakṛti in the sense of the latter's remaining in him in an undifferentiated way, but is regarded as the superintendent of dharma and adharma, and his agency is active only in the removal of obstacles, thereby helping the evolutionary process of prakṛti.

Thus Īśvara is distinguished from the Īśvara of Saṅkara Vedānta in this that there true existence is ascribed only to Īśvara, whereas all other forms and modes of Being are only regarded as illusory.

From what we have seen above it is clear that the main stress of the Yoga philosophy is on the method of samādhi. The knowledge that can be acquired by it differs from all other kinds of knowledge, ordinary perception, inference, etc., in this that it alone can bring objects before our mental eye with the clearest and most unerring light of comprehensibility in which the true nature of the thing is at once observed. Inferences and the words of scriptures are based on concepts or general notions of things. For the teaching of the Vedas is manifested in words ; and words are but names, terms or concepts formed by noting the general similarities of certain things and binding them down by a symbol. All deductive inferences are also based upon major propositions arrived at by inductive generalisations ; so it is easy to see that all knowledge that can be acquired by them is only generalised conceptions. Their process only represents the method by which the mind can pass from one generalised conception to another ; so the mind can in no way attain the knowledge of real things, absolute species, which are not the genus of any other thing ; so inference and scripture can only communicate to us the nature of the agreement or similarity of things and not the real things as they are. Ordinary perception also is not of much avail here, since it cannot bring within its scope subtle and fine things and things that are obstructed from the view of the senses. But samādhi has no such limitations and the knowledge that can be attained by it is absolutely unobstructed, true and real in the strictest sense of the terms.

Of all the points of difference between Yoga and Sāṃkhya the admission of Īśvara by the former and the emphasis given by it to the Yoga practice are the most important in distinguishing it from the latter. It seems probable that Īśvara was traditionally believed in the Yoga school to be a protector of the Yogins proceeding in their arduous course of complete self-control and absorptive concentration. The chances of a person adopting the course of Yoga practice for the attainment of success in this field does not depend only on the exertions of the Yogin, but upon the concurrence of many convenient circumstances such as physical fitness, freedom from illnesses and other obstacles. Faith in the patronage of God in favour of honest workers and believers served to pacify their minds and fill them with the cheerful hope and confidence which were so necessary for the success of Yoga practice. The metaphysical functions which are ascribed to Īśvara seem to be later additions for the sake of rendering his position more in harmony with the system. Mere faith in Iśvara for the practical benefit of the Yogins is thus interpreted by a reference to his superintendence of the development of cosmic evolution. Sāṃkhya relied largely on philosophical thinking leading to proper discrimination as to the difference between prakṛti and purusha which is the stage immediately antecedent to emancipation. There being thus no practical need for the admission of Īśvara, the theoretical need was also ignored and it was held that the inherent teleological purpose (*purushārthatā*) of prakṛti was sufficient to explain all the stages of cosmic evolution as well as its final separation from the purushas.

We have just seen that Sāṃkhya does not admit the existence of God, and considers that salvation can be obtained only by a steady perseverance in philosophical thinking, and does not put emphasis on the practical exercises which are regarded as essential by the Yoga. One other point of difference ought to be noted with regard to the conception of avidyā. According to Yoga, avidyā, as we have already explained it, means positive untrue beliefs such as believing the impure, uneternal, sorrow, and non-self to be the pure eternal, pleasure and the self respectively. With Sāṃkhya, however, avidyā is only the non-distinction of the difference between prakṛti and purusha. Both Sāṃkhya and Yoga admit that our bondage to prakṛti is due to an illusion or ignorance (avidyā), but Sāṃkhya holds the akhyāti theory which regards non-distinction of the difference as the cause of illusion whereas the Yoga holds the anyathākhyāti theory which regards positive misapprehension of the one as the other to be the cause of illusion. We have already referred to the difference in the course of the evolution of the categories as held by Sāṃkhya and Yoga. This also accounts for the difference between the technical terms of prakṛti, vikṛti and prakṛti-vikṛti of Sāṃkhya and the viśesha and aviśesha of the Yoga. The doctrine of dharma, lakshaṇa and avasthā-pariṇāma, though not in any way antagonistic to Sāṃkhya, is not so definitely described as in the Yoga. Some scholars think that Sāṃkhya did not believe in atoms as Yoga did. But though the word paramāṇu has not been mentioned in the *Kārikā*, it does not seem that Sāṃkhya did not believe in atoms ; and we have already noticed that Bhikshu considers the word sūkshma in *Kārikā* 39 as referring to the atoms. There are also slight differences with regard to the process involved in perception and this has been dealt with in my *Yoga philosophy in relation to other Indian systems of thought.** On almost all other fundamental points Sāṃkhya and Yoga are in complete agreement.

* Published as *Yoga Philosophy in Relation to other Systems of Indian Thought.*

CHAPTER XV

MATTER AND MIND

In conclusion it may be worth while saying a few words as to theories of the physical world supplementary to the views that have already been stated above.

Gross matter, as the possibility of sensation, has been divided into five classes, according to their relative grossness, corresponding to the relative grossness of the senses. Some modern investigators have tried to understand the five bhūtas, viz. ākāśa, marut, tejas, ap and kshiti as ether, gaseous heat and light, liquids and solids. But I cannot venture to agree when I reflect that solidity, liquidity and gaseousness represent only an impermanent aspect of matter. The division of matter from the standpoint of the possibility of our sensations, has a firm root in our nature as cognising beings and has therefore a better rational footing than the modern chemical division into elements and compounds, which are being daily threatened by the gradual advance of scientific culture. This carries with it no fixed and consistent rational conception as do the definitions of the ancients, but is a mere makeshift for understanding or representing certain chemical changes of matter and and has therefore a merely relative value.

There are five aspects from which gross matter can be viewed. These are (1) sthūla (gross), (2) svarūpa (substantive), (3) sūkshma (subtle), (4) anvaya (conjunction), (5) arthavattva (purpose for use). The sthūla or gross physical characteristics of the bhūtas are described as follows :—

Qualities of Earth—Form, heaviness, roughness, obstruction, stability, manifestation (vṛtti), difference, support, turbidity, hardness and enjoyability.

Ap—Smoothness, subtlety, clearness, whiteness, softness, heaviness, coolness, conservation, purity, cementation.

Tejas—Going upwards, cooking, burning, light, shining, dissipating, energising.

Vāyu—Transverse motion, purity, throwing, pushing, strength, movability, want of shadow.

Ākāśa—Motion in all directions, non-agglomeration, non-obstruction.

These physical characteristics are distinguished from the aspects by which they appeal to the senses, which are called their svarūpas. Earth is characterised by gandha or smell, ap by rasa or taste, tejas by rūpa, etc. Looked at from this point of view, we see that smell arises by the contact of the nasal organ with the hard particles of matter ; so this hardness or solidity which can so generate the sensibility of gandha, is said to be the svarūpa of kshiti. Taste can originate only in connection with liquidity, so this liquidity or sneha is the svarūpa or nature of ap. Light—the quality of visibility—manifests itself in connection with heat, so heat is the svarūpa of fire. The sensibility of touch is generated in connection with the vibration of air on the epidermal surface ; so this vibratory nature is the svarūpa of air.

The sensibility to sound proceeds from the nature of obstructionlessness, which belongs to akāśa, so this obstructionlessness is the svarūpa of ākāśa.

The third aspect is the aspect of tanmātras, which are the causes of the atoms or paramāṇus. Their fourth aspect is their aspect of guṇas or qualities of illumination, action, inertia. Their fifth aspect is that by which they are serviceable to purusha, by causing his pleasurable or painful experiences and finally his liberation.

Speaking of aggregation with regard to the structure of matter, we see that this is of two kinds (1) when the parts are in intimate union and fusion, e.g. any vegetable or animal body, the parts of which can never be considered separately. (2) When there are such mechanical aggregates or collocations of distinct and independent parts *yutasiddhāvayava* as the trees in a forest.

A dravya or substance is an aggregate of the former type, and is the grouping of generic or specific qualities and is not a separate entity—the abode of generic and specific qualities like the dravya of the Vaiśeshika conception. The aspect of an unification of generic and specific qualities seen in parts united in intimate union and fusion is called the dravya aspect. The aggregation of parts is the structural aspect of which the side of appearance is the unification of generic and specific qualities called the dravya.

The other aggregation of yutasiddhāvayava, i.e. the collocation of the distinct and independent parts, is again of two kinds, (1) in which stress may be laid on the distinction of parts, and (2) that in which stress is laid on their unity rather than on their distinctness. Thus in the expression mango-grove, we see that many mangoes make a grove, but the mangoes are not different from the grove. Here stress is laid on the aspect that mangoes are the same as the grove, which, however, is not the case when we say that here is a grove of mangoes, for the expression "grove of mangoes" clearly brings home to our minds the side of the distinct mango-trees which form a grove.

Of the gross elements, ākāśa seems especially to require a word of explanation. There are according to Vijñāna Bhikshu and Nāgeśa two kinds of ākāśa—kāraṇa (or primal) and kārya (atomic). The first or original is the undifferentiated formless tamas, for in that stage it has not the quality of manifesting itself in sounds. This kāraṇa later on develops into the atomic ākāśa, which has the property of sound. According to the conception of the purāṇas, this karyākāśa evolves from the ego as the first envelope of vāyu or air. The kāraṇakāśa or non-atomic ākāśa should not be considered as a mere vacuum, but must be conceived as a positive, all-pervasive entity, something like the ether of modern physicists.

From this ākāśa springs the atomic ākāśa or kāryākāśa, which is the cause of the manifestation of sound. All powers of hearing, even though they have their origin in the principle of egoism, reside in the ākāśa placed in the hollow of the ear. When soundness or defect is noticed therein, soundness or defect is also noticed in the power of hearing. Further, when of the sounds working in unison with the power of hearing, the sounds of solids, etc., are to be apprehended, then the power of hearing located in the hollow of the ear requires the capacity of resonance residing in the substratum of the ākāśa of the ear. This sense of hearing, then, operates when it is attracted by the sound originated and located in the mouth of the speaker, which acts as a loadstone. It is this ākāśa which gives penetrability to all bodies; in the absence of this, all bodies would be so compact that it would be difficult to pierce them even with a needle. In the *Sāṃkhya sūtrā* II. 12, it is said that eternal time and space are of the nature of ākāśa. So this so-called eternal time and space do not differ from the one undifferentiated formless tamas of which we have just spoken. Relative and infinite time arise from the motion of atoms in space—the cause of all change and transformation; and space as relative position cannot be better expressed than in the words of Dr. B. N. Seal, as "totality of positions as an order of co-existent points, and as such it is wholly relative to the understanding like order in time, being constructed on the basis of relations of position intuited by our empirical or relative consciousness. But there is this difference between space order and time order :—there is no unit of space as position (*dik*) though we may conceive time, as the moment (*kshaṇa*) regarded as the unit of change in the causal series. Spatial position (*dik*) results only from the different relations in which the all-pervasive ākāśa stands to the various finite objects. On the other hand, space as extension or locus of a finite body, or deśa, has an ultimate unit, being analysable into the infinitesimal extension quality inherent in the guṇas of prakṛti."*

Citta or mind has two degrees : (1) the form of states such as real cognition, including perception, inference, competent evidence, unreal cognition, imagination, sleep and memory. (2) In the form in which all those states are suppressed. Between the stage of complete outgoing activity of ordinary experience (*vyutthāna*) and complete suppression of all states, there are thousands of states of infinite variety, through which a man's experiences have to pass, from the vyutthāna state to the nirodha. In addition to the five states spoken of above, there is another kind of real knowledge and intuition, called prajñā, which dawns when by concentration the citta is fixed upon any one state and that alone. This prajñā is superior to all other means of knowledge, whether perception, inference or competent evidence of the Vedas, in this, that it is altogether unerring, unrestricted and unlimited in its scope.

Pramāṇa, we have seen, includes perception, inference and competent evidence. Perception originates when the mind or citta, through the senses (ear, skin, eye, taste and nose) is modified by external objects and passes to them, generating a kind of knowledge about them in which their specific characters become more predominant.

Mind is all-pervasive and can come in touch with the external world, by which we have the perception of the thing.

* Dr Ray's *Hindu Chemistry*, Vol. II, p. 81.

Like light, which emits rays and pervades all, though it remains in one place, the citta by its vṛttis comes in contact with the external world, is changed into the form of the object of perception and thus becomes the cause of perception; as the citta has to pass through the senses, it becomes coloured by them, which explains the fact that perception is impossible without the help of the senses. As it has to pass through the senses, it undergoes the limitations of the senses, which it can avoid, if it can directly concentrate itself upon any object without the help of the senses; from this originates the prajñā, through which dawns absolute real knowledge of the thing, unhampered by the limitations of the senses which can act only within a certain area or distance and cannot cognize subtler objects.

We see that in ordinary perception our minds are drawn towards the object, as iron is attracted by magnets. Thus Bhikshu says in explaining *Vyāsa-bhāshya* IV. 17 :—

" The objects of knowledge, though inactive in themselves, may yet draw the everchanging cittas towards them like a magnet and change them in accordance with their own forms, just as a piece of cloth is turned red by coming into contact with red lac." So it is that the cittas attain the form of anything with which they come in touch and there is then the perception that that thing is known. Perception (*pratyaksha*) is distinguished from inference, etc., in this, that here the knowledge arrived at is predominantly of the specific and special characters (*viśesha*) of the thing and not of its generic qualities as in inference, etc.

Inference proceeds from inference, and depends upon the fact that certain common qualities are found in all the members of a class, as distinguished from the members of a different class. Thus the qualities affirmed of a class will be found to exist in all the individual members of that class; this attribution of the generic characters of a class to the individual members that come under it is the essence of inference.

An object perceived or inferred by a competent man is described by him in words with the intention of transferring his knowledge to another; and the mental modification, which has for its sphere the meaning of such words, is the verbal cognition of the hearer. When the speaker has neither perceived nor inferred the object, and speaks of things which cannot be believed, the authority of verbal cognition fails. But it does not fail in the original speaker, God or Īśvara, and his dictates the Śāstras with reference either to the object of perception or of inference.

Viparyyaya or unreal cognition is the knowledge of the unreal as in doubt—a knowledge which possesses a form that does not tally with the real nature of the thing either as doubt or as false knowledge. Doubt may be illustrated by taking the case of a man who sees something in dim light and doubts its nature. "Is it a wooden post or a man?" In nature there is either the wooden post or the man, but there is no such fact or entity which corresponds with doubt: "Is it a wooden post or a man?" Knowledge as doubt is not cognition of a fact or entity. The illusion of seeing all things yellow through a defect of the eye (as in jaundice) can only be corrected when the objects are seen in their true colours. In doubt, however, their defective nature is at once manifest. Thus when we cannot be sure whether a certain thing is a post or a man, we know that our knowledge is not definite. So we have not to wait till the illusoriness of the previous knowledge is demonstrated by the advent of right knowledge. The evil nature of viparyyaya is exemplified in avidyā nescience, asmitā, rāga, etc.*

* Avidyā manifests itself in different forms: (1) as the afflictions (*kleśa*) of esmitā (agoism) rāga (attachment), dvesha (antipathy) and abhiniveśa (self-love); (2) as doubt and intellectual error; (3) as error of sense. All these manifestations of avidyā are also the different forms of

Viparyyaya is distinguished from vikalpa—imagination—in this, that though the latter is also unreal knowledge its nature as such is not demonstrated by any knowledge that follows, but is on the contrary admitted on all sides by the common consent of mankind. But it is only the learned who can demonstrate by arguments the illusoriness of vikalpa or imagination.

All class notions and concepts are formed by taking note only of the general characters of things and associating them with a symbol called "name." Things themselves, however, do not exist in the nature of these symbols or names or concepts; it is only an aspect of them that is diagrammatically represented by the intellect in the form of concepts. When concepts are united or separated in our thought and language, they consequently represent only an imaginary plane of knowledge, for the things are not as the concepts represent them. Thus when we say "Caitra's cow," it is only an imaginary relation for, strictly speaking, no such thing exists as the cow of Caitra. Caitra has no connection in reality with the cow. When we say purusha is of the nature of consciousness, there is the same illusory relation. Now what is here predicated of what? Purusha is consciousness itself, but in predication there must always be a statement of the relation of one to another. Thus it sometimes breaks a concept into two parts and predicates the one of the other, and sometimes predicates the unity of two concepts which are different. Thus

viparyyaya or bhrama (error, illusion, mistake). This bhrama in Yoga is the thinking of something as that which it is not (*anyathākhyāti*). Thus we think the miserable worldly existence as pleasurable and attribute the characteristics of prakṛti to purusha and vice versa. All afflictions are due to this confusion and misjudgment, the roots of which stay in the buddhis in all their transmigrations from one life to another. Sāṃkhya, however, differs from Yoga and thinks that all error (*avidyā* or *bhrama*) is due only to non-distinction between the true and the untrue. Thus non-distinction (*aviveka*) between prakṛti and purusha is the cause of all our miserable mundane existence. Avidyā and aviveka are thus synonymous with Sāṃkhya.

its sphere has a wide latitude in all thought-process conducted through language and involves an element of abstraction and construction which is called vikalpa. This represents the faculty by which our concepts are arranged in an analytical or synthetical proposition. It is said to be *śabdajñānānupāti vastuśūnyo vikalpaḥ*, i.e. the knowledge that springs from relating concepts or names, which relating does not actually exist in the objective world as it is represented in propositional forms.

Sleep is that mental state which has for its objective substratum the feeling of emptiness. It is called a state or notion of mind, for it is called back on awakening; when we feel that we have slept well our minds are clear, when we have slept badly our minds are listless, wandering and unsteady. For a person who seeks to attain communion or samādhi, these desires of sleep are to be suppressed, like all other desires. Memory is the retaining in the mind of objects perceived when perception occurs by the union of the cittas with external objects, according to the forms of which the cittas are transformed; it retains these perceptions, as impressions or saṃskāras by means of its inherent tamas. These saṃskāras generate memory, when such events occur as can manifest them by virtue of associations.

Thus memory comes when the percepts already known and acquired are kept in the mind in the form of impressions and are manifested by the udbodhakas or associative manifestors. It differs from perceptions in this that the latter are of the nature of perceiving the unknown and unperceived, whereas the former serves to bring before the mind percepts that have already been acquired. Memory is therefore of percepts already acquired by real cognition, unreal cognition, imagination, sleep and memory. It manifests itself in dreams as well as in waking states.

The relation between these states of mind and the saṃskāras

is this that their frequency and repetition strengthens the saṃskāras and thus ensures the revival of these states.

They are all endowed with sukha (pleasure), duḥkha (pain) and moha (ignorance). These feelings cannot be treated separately from the states themselves, for their manifestations are not different from the manifestation of the states themselves. Knowledge and feeling are but two different aspects of the modifications of cittas derived from prakṛti; hence neither can be thought separately from the other. The fusion of feeling with knowledge is therefore here more fundamental than in the modern tripartite division of mind.

In connection with this we are to consider the senses whose action on the external world is known as "perceiving," "grahaṇa," which is distinguished from "pratyaksha," which means the effect of "perceiving," viz. perception. Each sense has got its special sphere of work, e.g. sight is of the eye, and this is called their second aspect, viz. svarūpa. Their third aspect is of "asmitā" or ego, which manifests itself through the senses. Their fourth aspect is their characteristic of guṇas, viz. that of manifestation (*prakāśa*), action (*kriyā*) and retention (*sthiti*). Their fifth aspect is that they are set in motion for purusha, his experiences and liberation.

It is indeed difficult to find the relation of manas with the senses and the cittas. In more than one place manas is identified with cittas, and, on the other hand, it is described as a sense organ. There is another aspect in which manas is said to be the king of the cognitive and motor senses. Looked at in this aspect, manas is possibly the directive side of the ego by which it guides the cognitive and conative senses in the external world and is the cause of their harmonious activity for the experience of purusha. As a necessary attribute of this directive character of manas, the power of concentration, which is developed by prāṇāyāma, is said to belong to manas. This is the rajas side of manas.

There is another aspect of manas which is called the anuvyavasāya or reflection, by which the sensations (ālocana) are associated, differentiated, integrated, assimilated into percepts and concepts. This is possibly the sāttvika side of manas.

There is another aspect by which the percepts and concepts are retained (*dhāraṇa*) in the mind as saṃskāras, to be repeated or revealed again in the mind as actual states. This is the tamas side of manas.

In connection with this we may mention ūha (positive argumentation), apoha (negative argumentation) and tattvajñāna (logical conclusion) which are the modes of different anuvyavasāyas of the manas. Will, etc., are to be included with these (*Yoga-varttikā*, II. 18). Looked at from the point of view of cittas, these may equally be regarded as the modifications of cittas.

The motives which sustain this process of outgoing activity are false knowledge, and such other emotional elements as egoism, attachment, aversion, and love of life. These emotional elements remain in the mind in the germinal state as power alone ; or they exist in a fully operative state when a man is under the influence of any one of them ; or they alternate with others, such as attachment or aversion ; or they may become attenuated by meditation upon opposites. Accordingly they are called respectively prasupta, udāra, vicchinna or tanu. Man's minds or cittas may follow these outgoing states or experiences, or gradually remove those emotions which are commonly called afflictions, thus narrowing their sphere and proceeding towards final release.

All the psychic states described above, viz. pramāṇa, viparyyaya, etc., are called either afflicted or unafflicted according as they are moved towards outgoing activity or are actuated by the higher motive of emancipation by narrowing the field of experiences gradually to a smaller and smaller sphere and afterwards to suppress them altogether.

These two kinds of motives, one of afflictions that lead towards external objects of attachment and aversion or love of life, and the other which leads to striving for kaivalya, are the sole motives which guide all human actions and psychic states.

They influence us whenever suitable opportunities occur, so that by the study of the Vedas, self-criticism or right argumentation, or from the instruction of good men, abhyāsa and vairāgya may be roused by vidyā. Right knowledge and a tendency towards kaivalya may appear in the mind even when a man is immersed in the afflicted states of outgoing activity. So also afflicted states may appear when a man is bent upon or far advanced in those actions which are roused by vidyā or the tendency towards kaivalya.

It seems that the Yoga view of actions, or karma, does not deprive man of his freedom of will. The habit of performing particular types of action only strengthens the corresponding subconscious impressions or saṃskāras of those actual states, and thus makes it more and more difficult to overcome their propensity to generate their corresponding actual states, and thus obstructs the adoption of an unhampered and free course of action. The other limitation to the scope of the activity of his free will is the vāsanā aspect of the saṃskāras by which he naturally feels himself attached by pleasurable ties to certain experiences and by painful ones to others. But these only represent the difficulties and impediments which come to a man, when he has to adopt the Yoga course of life, the contrary of which he might have been practising for a very long period, extending over many life-states.

The free will is not curbed in any way, for it follows directly from the teleological purpose of prakṛti, which moves for the experience and liberation of purusha. So this motive of liberation, which is the basis of all good conduct, can never be subordinated to the other impulse, which goads man towards outgoing experiences. But, on the other hand, this original impulse which attracts man towards these ordinary experiences, as it is due to the false knowledge which identifies prakṛti with purusha, becomes itself subordinate and loses its influence and power, when such events occur, which nullify false knowledge by tending to produce a vision of the true knowledge of the relation of prakṛti with purusha. Thus, for example, if by the grace of God false knowledge (avidyā) is removed, true knowledge at once dawns upon the mind and all the afflictions lose their power.

Free-will and responsibility for action cease in those life-states which are intended for suffering from actions only, e.g. life-states of insects, etc.

APPENDIX

SPHOṬAVĀDA

ANOTHER point to be noted in connection with the main metaphysical theories of Patañjali is the Sphoṭa theory which considers the relation of words with their ideas and the things which they signify. Generally these three are not differentiated one from the other, and we are not accustomed to distinguish them from one another. Though distinct yet they are often identified or taken in one act of thought, by a sort of illusion. The nature of this illusory process comes to our view when we consider the process of auditory perception of words. Thus if we follow the *Bhāshya* as explained by Vijñāna Bhikshu we find that by an effect of our organs of speech, the letters are pronounced. This vocal sound is produced in the mouth of the speaker from which place the sound moves in aerial waves until it reaches the ear drum of the hearer, by coming in contact with which it produces the audible sound called dhvani (*Yoga-vārttika*, III. 17). The special modifications of this dhvani are seen to be generated in the form of letters (*varṇa*) and the general name for these modifications is nāda. This sound as it exists in the stage of varṇas or letters is also called varṇa. If we apply the word śabda or sound in the most general sense, then we can say that this is the second stage of sound moving towards word-cognition, the first stage being that of its utterance in the mouth of the speaker. The third stage of śabda is that in which the letters, for example, g, au, and ḥ, of the word "gauḥ" are taken together and the complete word-form "gauḥ" comes before our view. The comprehension of this complete word-form is an attribute of the mind and not of the sense of hearing. For the sense of hearing senses the letter-forms of the sound one by one as the particular letters are pronounced by the speaker and as they approach the ear one by one in air-waves. But each letter-form sound vanishes as it is generated, for the sense of hearing has no power to hold them together and comprehend the letter-forms as forming a complete word-form. The ideation of this complete word-form in the mind is called sphoṭa. It differs from the letter-form in this that it is a complete, inseparable, and unified whole, devoid of any past, and thus is quite unlike the letter-forms which die the next moment after they originate. According to the system of Patañjali as explained by the commentators, all significance belongs to this sphoṭa-form and never to the letters pronounced or heard. Letters when they are pronounced and heard in a particular order serve to give rise to such complete ideational word-images which possess some denotation and connotation of meaning and are thus called "sphoṭas," or that which illuminates. These are essentially different in nature from the sounds in letter-forms generated in the senses of hearing which are momentary and evanescent and can never be brought together to form one whole, have no meaning, and have the sense of hearing as their seat.

The Vaiśeshika view.—Saṅkara Miśra, however, holds that this "sphoṭa" theory is absolutely unnecessary, for even the supporters of sphoṭa agree that the sphoṭa stands conventionally for the thing that it signifies; now if that be the case what is the good of admitting sphoṭa at all? It is better to say that the conventionality of names belongs to the letters themselves, which by virtue of that can conjointly signify a thing; and it is when you look at the letters from this aspect—their unity with reference to their denotation of one thing

—that you call them a pada or name (*Upaskāra*, II. 2, 21). So according to this view we find that there is no existence of a different entity called "name" or "sphoṭa" which can be distinguished from the letters coming in a definite order within the range of the sense of hearing. The letters pronounced and heard in a definite order are jointly called a name when they denote a particular meaning or object.

Kumārila's view:—Kumārila, the celebrated scholar of the Mīmāṃsa school, also denies the sphoṭa theory and asserts like the Vaiśeshika that the significance belongs to the letters themselves and not to any special sphoṭa or name. To prove this he first proves that the letter-forms are stable and eternal and suffer no change on account of the differences in their modes of accent and pronunciation. He then goes on to show that the sphoṭa view only serves to increase the complexity without any attendant advantage. Thus the objection that applies to the so-called defect of the letter-denotation theory that the letters cannot together denote a thing since they do not do it individually, applies to the name-denotation of the sphoṭa theory, since there also it is said that though there is no sphoṭa or name corresponding to each letter yet the letters conjointly give rise to a sphoṭa or complete name (*Ślokavārttika*, Sphoṭavāda, śl. 91–93).

The letters, however, are helped by their potencies (saṃskāras) in denoting the object, or the meaning. The sphoṭa theory has, according to Kumārila and Pārthasārathi, also to admit this saṃskāra of the letters in the manifestation of the name or the śabda-sphoṭa, whereas they only admit it as the operating power of the letters in denoting the object or the thing signified. Saṃskāras according to Kumārila are thus admitted both by the sphoṭa theorists and the Kumārila school of Mīmāṃsa, only with this difference that the latter with its help can directly denote the object of the signified, whereas the former have only to go a step backwards in thinking their saṃskāra to give rise to the name or the śabda-sphoṭa alone (*Nyāyaratnākara*, Sphoṭavāda, śl. 104).

Kumārila says that he takes great pains to prove the nullity of the sphoṭa theory only because if the sphoṭa view be accepted then it comes to the same thing as saying that words and letters have no validity, so that all actions depending on them also come to lose their validity (*Ślokavārttika*, Sphoṭavāda, śl. 137).

Prabhākara.—Prabhākara also holds the same view; for according to him also the letters are pronounced in a definite order; though when individually considered they are momentary and evanescent, yet they maintain themselves by their potency in the form of a pāda or name, and thus signify an object. Thus Śāliknātha Miśra says in his *Prakaraṇa Pañcikā*, p. 89: "It is reasonable to suppose that since the later letters in a word are dependent upon the perception of a preceding one some special change is wrought in the letters themselves which leads to the comprehension of the meaning of a word. . . . It cannot be proved either by perception or by inference that there is any word apart from the letters; the word has thus for its constituents the letters."

Śabara.—The views of Kamārila and Prahhākara thus explicated are but elaborate explanations of the view of Śabara who states the whole theory in a single line—*pūrvavarṇa-janitasaṃskārasahito'ntyo varṇaḥ pratyāyakaḥ.*

"The last letter together with the potency generated by the preceding letters is the cause of significance."

Mahābhāshya and Kaiyaṭa.—After describing the view of those who are antagonistic to the sphoṭa theory it is necessary to mention the Vaiākaraṇa school which is in favour of it; thus we find that in explaining the following passage of Mahābhāshya,

"What is then a word? It is that which being pronounced

one can understand specific objects such as those (cows) which have tail, hoofs, horns, etc."

Kaiyata says: "The grammarians think that denotation belongs to words, as distinct from letters which are pronounced, for if each of the letters should denote the object, there would be no need of pronouncing the succeeding letters. . . ."

The vaiyakaraṇas admit the significant force of names as distinguished from letters. For if the significant force be attributed to letters individually, then the first letter being quite sufficient to signify the object, the utterance of other letters becomes unnecessary; and according to this view if it is held that each letter has the generating power, then also they cannot do it simultaneously, since they are uttered one after another. On the view of manifestation, also, since the letters are manifested one after another, they cannot be collected together in due order; if their existence in memory is sufficient, then we should expect no difference of signification or meaning by the change of order in the utterance of the letters; that is "*sara*" ought to have the same meaning as "*rasa*." So it must be admitted that the power of signification belongs to the sphoṭa as manifested by the nādas as has been described in detail in *Vākyapadīya*.

As the relation between the perceiving capacity and the object of perception is a constant one so also is the relation between the sphoṭa and the nāda as the manifested and the manifestor (*Vākyapadīya* 98). Just as the image varies corresponding to the variation of the reflector, as oil, water, etc., so also the reflected or manifested image differs according to the difference of the manifestor (*Vāk.* 100). Though the manifestation of letters, propositions and names occurs at one and the same time yet there seems to be a "before and after" according to the "before and after" of the nāda utterances (*Vāk.* 102). That which is produced through the union and disunion (of nādas or dhvanis) is called sphoṭa, whereas other sound-perceptions arising from sounds are called dhvanis (*Vāk.* 103). As by the movement of water the image of a thing situated elsewhere also appears to adopt the movement of the water and thus seems to move, so also the sphoṭa, though unchanging in itself, yet appears to suffer change in accordance with the change of nāda which manifests it (*Vāk.* 49). As there are no parts of the letters themselves so the letters also do not exist as parts of the name. There is again no ultimate or real difference between names and propositions (*Vāk.* 73). It is only in popular usage that they are regarded as different. That which others regard as the most important thing is regarded as false here, for propositions only are here regarded as valid (*Vāk.* 74). Though the letters which manifest names and propositions are altogether different from them, yet their powers often appear as quite undifferentiated from them (*Vāk.* 89). Thus when propositions are manifested by the cause of the manifestation of propositions they appear to consist of parts when they first appear before the mind. Thus, though the pada-sphoṭa or the vākya-sphoṭa does not really consist of parts, yet, as the powers of letters cannot often be differentiated from them, they also appear frequently to be made up of parts (*Vāk.* 91).

The Yoga View.—As to the relation of the letters to the sphoṭa, Vācaspati says, in explaining the *Bhāshya,* that each of the letters has the potentiality of manifesting endless meanings, but none of them can do so individually; it is only when the letter-form sounds are pronounced in succession by one effort of speech that the individual letters by their own particular contiguity or distance from one another can manifest a complete word called the sphoṭa. Thus owing to the variation of contiguity of distance by intervention from other letter-form sounds any letter-form sound may manifest any meaning or word; for the particular order and the association of letter-form sounds depend upon the particular output of energy required in uttering them. The sphoṭa is thus a particular modification of buddhi, whereas the letter-form sounds have their origin in the organ of speech when they are uttered, and the sense of hearing when they are heard. It is well to note here that the theory that the letters themselves have endless potentiality and can manifest any word-sphoṭas, according to their particular combinations and re-combinations, is quite in keeping with the main metaphysical doctrine of the Pātañjala theory.

Vākya-sphoṭa.—What is said here of the letter-form sounds and the śabda-sphoṭas also applies to the relation that the śabda-sphoṭas bear to propositions or sentences. A word or name does not stand alone; it always exists as combined with other words in the form of a proposition. Thus the word "tree" whenever it is pronounced carries with it the notion of a verb "asti" or "exists," and thereby demonstrates its meaning. The single word "tree" without any reference to any other word which can give it a propositional form has no meaning. Knowledge of words always comes in propositional forms; just as different letter-form sounds demonstrate by their mutual collocation a single word or śabda-sphoṭa, so the words also by their mutual combination or collocation demonstrate judgmental or propositional significance or meaning. As the letters themselves have no meaning so the words themselves have also no meaning; it is only by placing them side by side in a particular order that a meaning dawns in the mind. When single words are pronounced they associate other words with themselves and thus appear to signify a meaning. But though a single word is sufficient by association with other words to carry a meaning, yet sentences or propositions should not be deemed unnecessary for they serve to specialise that meaning (*niyamārthe anuvādaḥ*). Thus "cooks" means that any subject makes something the object of his cooking. The mention of the subject "Devadatta" and the object "rice" only specialises the subject and the object. Though the analysis of a sentence into the words of which it is constituted is as imaginary as the analysis of a word into the letter-form sounds, it is generally done in order to get an analytical view of the meaning of a sentence—an imaginary division of it as into cases, verbs, etc.

Abhihitānvayavada and Anvitābhidhānavāda.—This reminds us of the two very famous theories about the relation of sentences to words, viz. the "Abhihitānvayavāda" and the "Anvitābhidhānavāda." The former means that words themselves can express their separate meanings by the function abhidhā or denotation; these are subsequently combined into a sentence expressing one connected idea. The latter means that words only express a meaning as parts of a sentence, and as grammatically connected with each other; they only express an action or something connected with action; in "sāmānaya" "bring the cow"—"gām" does not properly mean "gotva" but "ānayanānvitagotva," that is, the bovine genus as connected with bringing. We cannot have a case of a noun without some governing verb and vice versa—(Sarvadarśana-saṃgraha, Cowell).

The Yoga point of view.—It will be seen that strictly speaking the Yoga view does not agree with any one of these views though it approaches nearer to the Anvitābhidhāna view than to the Abhihitānvaya view. For according to the Yoga view the idea of the sentence is the only true thing; words only serve to manifest this idea but have themselves no meaning. The division of a sentence into the component word-conceptions is only an imaginary analysis—an afterthought.

Confusion the cause of verbal cognition.—According to Patañjali's view verbal cognition proceeds only from a confusion of the letter-form sounds (which are perceived in the sense of hearing), the śabda-sphoṭa which is manifested in the buddhi, and the object which exists in the external world. These three though altogether distinct from one another yet appear to be unified on account of the saṅketa or sign, so that the letter-form sounds, the śabda-sphoṭa, and the thing, can never be distinguished from one another. Of course knowledge can arise even in those cases where there is no actual external object, simply by virtue of the manifesting power of the letter-form sounds. This saṅketa is again defined as the confusion of words and their meanings through memory, so that it appears that what a word is, so is its denoted object, and what a denoted word is, so is its object. Convention is a manifestation of memory of the nature of mutual confusion of words and their meanings. This object is the same as this word, and this word is the same as this object. Thus there is no actual unity of words and their objects: such unity is imaginary and due to beginningless tradition. This view may well be contrasted with Nyāya, according to which the convention of works as signifying objects is due to the will of God.

INDEX

Theories, 2
Thing, 150
Thing-in-itself, 2, 37
Thought, 2
Time, 79, 139, 152, 169 ; as discrete moments, 44 ; as unit of change, 43 ; element of imagination in, 44, unit of, 46 ; order, 170
Tinduka, 77
Trance, 135, 136, 143 ; Trance-cognition, 95
Transcendent, 18
Transformations, 20, 24
trasareṇu, 66
triguṇamaviveki vishayaḥ sāmānyamacetanaṃ prasavadharmi vyaktaṃ tathā pradhānaṃ tadviparītastathā pumān, 42
Truth, 141
Truthfulness, 139, 140, 144
Tulyajātīyātulyajātīyaśaktibhedānupātinaḥ, 6

udāra, 176
udbodhaka, 174
udghāta, 146, 147
udita, 73
Ultimate state, 7
Unafflicted, 176
Understanding, 19
Undetermined, 8
Undifferentiated, 12, 162
Unindividuated, 12
Universe, 1, 13 ; a product of guṇa combinations, 37
Unknowable, 2, 37
Unmanifested, 4, 8, 72
Unmediated, 8
Unpredicable, 73
Unreal, 28
Unspecialised, 7
Unwisdom, 142
Upanishads, 11
upastha, 54, 58
upādāna, 61
upādāna kāraṇa, 61, 133
upekshā, 137, 139
utpādyakāraṇa, 135
uttaradeśa, 43 n.
ūha, 101, 176

vaikārika, 56
vairāgya, 100, 101, 127, 129, 130, 135, 136, 143, 149, 162, 177
Vaiśeshika, 43 n., 71, 168
Vaiśeshika atoms, 70
vaishṇava, 10
Vanity, 143
vaśīkāra, 128
vastupatitaḥ, 44
vastusāmye cittabhedāt tayor vibhaktaḥ panthāḥ, 35 n.
Vācaspati, 3, 5 n., 8, 12, 32, 33, 35, 44, 46 n., 51, 55, 62, 65, 66, 67, 75, 78, 87, 89, 93, 109, 110, 112, 118, 126, 129, 144, 153, 154
vāk, 54
Vākyapadīya, 183
vāsanā, 99, 106, 108, 114, 116, 177 ; contrasted with karmāśaya, 107
Vāyu, 167
Vāyu atom, 65
Vedas, 154, 160, 162, 170, 177
Vedānta, 11, 14, 24, 27, 28, 29, 162
Vedāntism, 14
Vedāntists, 12, 26, 66, 81
Vedic, 103
Vehicles of actions, 103
Venkaṭa, 10
Veracity, 136, 140
Verbal cognition, cause of, 186 view of Nyāya, 187
vibhu, 43 n.
vibhu parimāṇa, 29 n.
vibhūti, 158
Vibhūtipāda, 22
vicāra, 153
vicārānugata, 125, 153
vicchinna, 176
Vice, 86, 87
videha, 127
vidyā, 177
vidyāviparītam jñānāntaraṃ avidyā, 11, 97
Vijñanāmṛta-bhāshya, 88, 90
Vijñāna Bhikshu, 4, 15
vikalpa, 101, 150, 173, 174
vikārakāraṇa, 133
vikāryyakāraṇa, 135
vikṛti, 7 n., 165

A CATALOG OF SELECTED

DOVER BOOKS

IN ALL FIELDS OF INTEREST

A CATALOG OF SELECTED DOVER BOOKS IN ALL FIELDS OF INTEREST

STICKLEY CRAFTSMAN FURNITURE CATALOGS, Gustav Stickley and L. & J. G. Stickley. Beautiful, functional furniture in two authentic catalogs from 1910. 594 illustrations, including 277 photos, show settles, rockers, armchairs, reclining chairs, bookcases, desks, tables. 183pp. 6½ x 9¼. 23838-5

AMERICAN LOCOMOTIVES IN HISTORIC PHOTOGRAPHS: 1858 to 1949, Ron Ziel (ed.). A rare collection of 126 meticulously detailed official photographs, called "builder portraits," of American locomotives that majestically chronicle the rise of steam locomotive power in America. Introduction. Detailed captions. xi+ 129pp. 9 x 12. 27393-8

AMERICA'S LIGHTHOUSES: An Illustrated History, Francis Ross Holland, Jr. Delightfully written, profusely illustrated fact-filled survey of over 200 American lighthouses since 1716. History, anecdotes, technological advances, more. 240pp. 8 x 10¾. 25576-X

TOWARDS A NEW ARCHITECTURE, Le Corbusier. Pioneering manifesto by founder of "International School." Technical and aesthetic theories, views of industry, economics, relation of form to function, "mass-production split" and much more. Profusely illustrated. 320pp. 6⅛ x 9¼. (Available in U.S. only.) 25023-7

HOW THE OTHER HALF LIVES, Jacob Riis. Famous journalistic record, exposing poverty and degradation of New York slums around 1900, by major social reformer. 100 striking and influential photographs. 233pp. 10 x 7⅞. 22012-5

FRUIT KEY AND TWIG KEY TO TREES AND SHRUBS, William M. Harlow. One of the handiest and most widely used identification aids. Fruit key covers 120 deciduous and evergreen species; twig key 160 deciduous species. Easily used. Over 300 photographs. 126pp. 5⅜ x 8½. 20511-8

COMMON BIRD SONGS, Dr. Donald J. Borror. Songs of 60 most common U.S. birds: robins, sparrows, cardinals, bluejays, finches, more–arranged in order of increasing complexity. Up to 9 variations of songs of each species.
Cassette and manual 99911-4

ORCHIDS AS HOUSE PLANTS, Rebecca Tyson Northen. Grow cattleyas and many other kinds of orchids–in a window, in a case, or under artificial light. 63 illustrations. 148pp. 5⅜ x 8½. 23261-1

MONSTER MAZES, Dave Phillips. Masterful mazes at four levels of difficulty. Avoid deadly perils and evil creatures to find magical treasures. Solutions for all 32 exciting illustrated puzzles. 48pp. 8¼ x 11. 26005-4

MOZART'S DON GIOVANNI (DOVER OPERA LIBRETTO SERIES), Wolfgang Amadeus Mozart. Introduced and translated by Ellen H. Bleiler. Standard Italian libretto, with complete English translation. Convenient and thoroughly portable–an ideal companion for reading along with a recording or the performance itself. Introduction. List of characters. Plot summary. 121pp. 5¼ x 8½. 24944-1

TECHNICAL MANUAL AND DICTIONARY OF CLASSICAL BALLET, Gail Grant. Defines, explains, comments on steps, movements, poses and concepts. 15-page pictorial section. Basic book for student, viewer. 127pp. 5⅜ x 8½. 21843-0

THE CLARINET AND CLARINET PLAYING, David Pino. Lively, comprehensive work features suggestions about technique, musicianship, and musical interpretation, as well as guidelines for teaching, making your own reeds, and preparing for public performance. Includes an intriguing look at clarinet history. "A godsend," *The Clarinet*, Journal of the International Clarinet Society. Appendixes. 7 illus. 320pp. 5⅜ x 8½. 40270-3

HOLLYWOOD GLAMOR PORTRAITS, John Kobal (ed.). 145 photos from 1926-49. Harlow, Gable, Bogart, Bacall; 94 stars in all. Full background on photographers, technical aspects. 160pp. 8⅜ x 11¼. 23352-9

THE ANNOTATED CASEY AT THE BAT: A Collection of Ballads about the Mighty Casey/Third, Revised Edition, Martin Gardner (ed.). Amusing sequels and parodies of one of America's best loved poems: Casey's Revenge, Why Casey Whiffed, Casey's Sister at the Bat, others. 256pp. 5⅜ x 8½. 28598-7

THE RAVEN AND OTHER FAVORITE POEMS, Edgar Allan Poe. Over 40 of the author's most memorable poems: "The Bells," "Ulalume," "Israfel," "To Helen," "The Conqueror Worm," "Eldorado," "Annabel Lee," many more. Alphabetic lists of titles and first lines. 64pp. 5$\frac{3}{16}$ x 8¼. 26685-0

PERSONAL MEMOIRS OF U. S. GRANT, Ulysses Simpson Grant. Intelligent, deeply moving firsthand account of Civil War campaigns, considered by many the finest military memoirs ever written. Includes letters, historic photographs, maps and more. 528pp. 6⅛ x 9¼. 28587-1

ANCIENT EGYPTIAN MATERIALS AND INDUSTRIES, A. Lucas and J. Harris. Fascinating, comprehensive, thoroughly documented text describes this ancient civilization's vast resources and the processes that incorporated them in daily life, including the use of animal products, building materials, cosmetics, perfumes and incense, fibers, glazed ware, glass and its manufacture, materials used in the mummification process, and much more. 544pp. 6⅛ x 9¼. (Available in U.S. only.) 40446-3

RUSSIAN STORIES/RUSSKIE RASSKAZY: A Dual-Language Book, edited by Gleb Struve. Twelve tales by such masters as Chekhov, Tolstoy, Dostoevsky, Pushkin, others. Excellent word-for-word English translations on facing pages, plus teaching and study aids, Russian/English vocabulary, biographical/critical introductions, more. 416pp. 5⅜ x 8½. 26244-8

PHILADELPHIA THEN AND NOW: 60 Sites Photographed in the Past and Present, Kenneth Finkel and Susan Oyama. Rare photographs of City Hall, Logan Square, Independence Hall, Betsy Ross House, other landmarks juxtaposed with contemporary views. Captures changing face of historic city. Introduction. Captions. 128pp. 8¼ x 11. 25790-8

AIA ARCHITECTURAL GUIDE TO NASSAU AND SUFFOLK COUNTIES, LONG ISLAND, The American Institute of Architects, Long Island Chapter, and the Society for the Preservation of Long Island Antiquities. Comprehensive, well-researched and generously illustrated volume brings to life over three centuries of Long Island's great architectural heritage. More than 240 photographs with authoritative, extensively detailed captions. 176pp. 8¼ x 11. 26946-9

NORTH AMERICAN INDIAN LIFE: Customs and Traditions of 23 Tribes, Elsie Clews Parsons (ed.). 27 fictionalized essays by noted anthropologists examine religion, customs, government, additional facets of life among the Winnebago, Crow, Zuni, Eskimo, other tribes. 480pp. 6⅛ x 9¼. 27377-6

FRANK LLOYD WRIGHT'S DANA HOUSE, Donald Hoffmann. Pictorial essay of residential masterpiece with over 160 interior and exterior photos, plans, elevations, sketches and studies. 128pp. 9¼ x 10¾. 29120-0

THE MALE AND FEMALE FIGURE IN MOTION: 60 Classic Photographic Sequences, Eadweard Muybridge. 60 true-action photographs of men and women walking, running, climbing, bending, turning, etc., reproduced from rare 19th-century masterpiece. vi + 121pp. 9 x 12. 24745-7

1001 QUESTIONS ANSWERED ABOUT THE SEASHORE, N. J. Berrill and Jacquelyn Berrill. Queries answered about dolphins, sea snails, sponges, starfish, fishes, shore birds, many others. Covers appearance, breeding, growth, feeding, much more. 305pp. 5¼ x 8¼. 23366-9

ATTRACTING BIRDS TO YOUR YARD, William J. Weber. Easy-to-follow guide offers advice on how to attract the greatest diversity of birds: birdhouses, feeders, water and waterers, much more. 96pp. 5³⁄₁₆ x 8¼. 28927-3

MEDICINAL AND OTHER USES OF NORTH AMERICAN PLANTS: A Historical Survey with Special Reference to the Eastern Indian Tribes, Charlotte Erichsen-Brown. Chronological historical citations document 500 years of usage of plants, trees, shrubs native to eastern Canada, northeastern U.S. Also complete identifying information. 343 illustrations. 544pp. 6½ x 9¼. 25951-X

STORYBOOK MAZES, Dave Phillips. 23 stories and mazes on two-page spreads: Wizard of Oz, Treasure Island, Robin Hood, etc. Solutions. 64pp. 8¼ x 11. 23628-5

AMERICAN NEGRO SONGS: 230 Folk Songs and Spirituals, Religious and Secular, John W. Work. This authoritative study traces the African influences of songs sung and played by black Americans at work, in church, and as entertainment. The author discusses the lyric significance of such songs as "Swing Low, Sweet Chariot," "John Henry," and others and offers the words and music for 230 songs. Bibliography. Index of Song Titles. 272pp. 6½ x 9¼. 40271-1

MOVIE-STAR PORTRAITS OF THE FORTIES, John Kobal (ed.). 163 glamor, studio photos of 106 stars of the 1940s: Rita Hayworth, Ava Gardner, Marlon Brando, Clark Gable, many more. 176pp. 8⅜ x 11¼. 23546-7

BENCHLEY LOST AND FOUND, Robert Benchley. Finest humor from early 30s, about pet peeves, child psychologists, post office and others. Mostly unavailable elsewhere. 73 illustrations by Peter Arno and others. 183pp. 5⅜ x 8½. 22410-4

YEKL and THE IMPORTED BRIDEGROOM AND OTHER STORIES OF YIDDISH NEW YORK, Abraham Cahan. Film Hester Street based on *Yekl* (1896). Novel, other stories among first about Jewish immigrants on N.Y.'s East Side. 240pp. 5⅜ x 8½. 22427-9

SELECTED POEMS, Walt Whitman. Generous sampling from *Leaves of Grass*. Twenty-four poems include "I Hear America Singing," "Song of the Open Road," "I Sing the Body Electric," "When Lilacs Last in the Dooryard Bloom'd," "O Captain! My Captain!"–all reprinted from an authoritative edition. Lists of titles and first lines. 128pp. 5³⁄₁₆ x 8¼. 26878-0

THE BEST TALES OF HOFFMANN, E. T. A. Hoffmann. 10 of Hoffmann's most important stories: "Nutcracker and the King of Mice," "The Golden Flowerpot," etc. 458pp. 5⅜ x 8½. 21793-0

FROM FETISH TO GOD IN ANCIENT EGYPT, E. A. Wallis Budge. Rich detailed survey of Egyptian conception of "God" and gods, magic, cult of animals, Osiris, more. Also, superb English translations of hymns and legends. 240 illustrations. 545pp. 5⅜ x 8½. 25803-3

FRENCH STORIES/CONTES FRANÇAIS: A Dual-Language Book, Wallace Fowlie. Ten stories by French masters, Voltaire to Camus: "Micromegas" by Voltaire; "The Atheist's Mass" by Balzac; "Minuet" by de Maupassant; "The Guest" by Camus, six more. Excellent English translations on facing pages. Also French-English vocabulary list, exercises, more. 352pp. 5⅜ x 8½. 26443-2

CHICAGO AT THE TURN OF THE CENTURY IN PHOTOGRAPHS: 122 Historic Views from the Collections of the Chicago Historical Society, Larry A. Viskochil. Rare large-format prints offer detailed views of City Hall, State Street, the Loop, Hull House, Union Station, many other landmarks, circa 1904-1913. Introduction. Captions. Maps. 144pp. 9⅜ x 12¼. 24656-6

OLD BROOKLYN IN EARLY PHOTOGRAPHS, 1865-1929, William Lee Younger. Luna Park, Gravesend race track, construction of Grand Army Plaza, moving of Hotel Brighton, etc. 157 previously unpublished photographs. 165pp. 8⅞ x 11¾. 23587-4

THE MYTHS OF THE NORTH AMERICAN INDIANS, Lewis Spence. Rich anthology of the myths and legends of the Algonquins, Iroquois, Pawnees and Sioux, prefaced by an extensive historical and ethnological commentary. 36 illustrations. 480pp. 5⅜ x 8½. 25967-6

AN ENCYCLOPEDIA OF BATTLES: Accounts of Over 1,560 Battles from 1479 B.C. to the Present, David Eggenberger. Essential details of every major battle in recorded history from the first battle of Megiddo in 1479 B.C. to Grenada in 1984. List of Battle Maps. New Appendix covering the years 1967-1984. Index. 99 illustrations. 544pp. 6½ x 9¼. 24913-1

SAILING ALONE AROUND THE WORLD, Captain Joshua Slocum. First man to sail around the world, alone, in small boat. One of great feats of seamanship told in delightful manner. 67 illustrations. 294pp. 5⅜ x 8½. 20326-3

ANARCHISM AND OTHER ESSAYS, Emma Goldman. Powerful, penetrating, prophetic essays on direct action, role of minorities, prison reform, puritan hypocrisy, violence, etc. 271pp. 5⅜ x 8½. 22484-8

MYTHS OF THE HINDUS AND BUDDHISTS, Ananda K. Coomaraswamy and Sister Nivedita. Great stories of the epics; deeds of Krishna, Shiva, taken from puranas, Vedas, folk tales; etc. 32 illustrations. 400pp. 5⅜ x 8½. 21759-0

THE TRAUMA OF BIRTH, Otto Rank. Rank's controversial thesis that anxiety neurosis is caused by profound psychological trauma which occurs at birth. 256pp. 5⅜ x 8½. 27974-X

A THEOLOGICO-POLITICAL TREATISE, Benedict Spinoza. Also contains unfinished Political Treatise. Great classic on religious liberty, theory of government on common consent. R. Elwes translation. Total of 421pp. 5⅜ x 8½. 20249-6

MY BONDAGE AND MY FREEDOM, Frederick Douglass. Born a slave, Douglass became outspoken force in antislavery movement. The best of Douglass' autobiographies. Graphic description of slave life. 464pp. 5⅜ x 8½. 22457-0

FOLLOWING THE EQUATOR: A Journey Around the World, Mark Twain. Fascinating humorous account of 1897 voyage to Hawaii, Australia, India, New Zealand, etc. Ironic, bemused reports on peoples, customs, climate, flora and fauna, politics, much more. 197 illustrations. 720pp. 5⅜ x 8½. 26113-1

THE PEOPLE CALLED SHAKERS, Edward D. Andrews. Definitive study of Shakers: origins, beliefs, practices, dances, social organization, furniture and crafts, etc. 33 illustrations. 351pp. 5⅜ x 8½. 21081-2

THE MYTHS OF GREECE AND ROME, H. A. Guerber. A classic of mythology, generously illustrated, long prized for its simple, graphic, accurate retelling of the principal myths of Greece and Rome, and for its commentary on their origins and significance. With 64 illustrations by Michelangelo, Raphael, Titian, Rubens, Canova, Bernini and others. 480pp. 5⅜ x 8½. 27584-1

PSYCHOLOGY OF MUSIC, Carl E. Seashore. Classic work discusses music as a medium from psychological viewpoint. Clear treatment of physical acoustics, auditory apparatus, sound perception, development of musical skills, nature of musical feeling, host of other topics. 88 figures. 408pp. 5⅜ x 8½. 21851-1

THE PHILOSOPHY OF HISTORY, Georg W. Hegel. Great classic of Western thought develops concept that history is not chance but rational process, the evolution of freedom. 457pp. 5⅜ x 8½. 20112-0

THE BOOK OF TEA, Kakuzo Okakura. Minor classic of the Orient: entertaining, charming explanation, interpretation of traditional Japanese culture in terms of tea ceremony. 94pp. 5⅜ x 8½. 20070-1

LIFE IN ANCIENT EGYPT, Adolf Erman. Fullest, most thorough, detailed older account with much not in more recent books, domestic life, religion, magic, medicine, commerce, much more. Many illustrations reproduce tomb paintings, carvings, hieroglyphs, etc. 597pp. 5⅜ x 8½. 22632-8

SUNDIALS, Their Theory and Construction, Albert Waugh. Far and away the best, most thorough coverage of ideas, mathematics concerned, types, construction, adjusting anywhere. Simple, nontechnical treatment allows even children to build several of these dials. Over 100 illustrations. 230pp. 5⅜ x 8½. 22947-5

THEORETICAL HYDRODYNAMICS, L. M. Milne-Thomson. Classic exposition of the mathematical theory of fluid motion, applicable to both hydrodynamics and aerodynamics. Over 600 exercises. 768pp. 6⅛ x 9¼. 68970-0

SONGS OF EXPERIENCE: Facsimile Reproduction with 26 Plates in Full Color, William Blake. 26 full-color plates from a rare 1826 edition. Includes "The Tyger," "London," "Holy Thursday," and other poems. Printed text of poems. 48pp. 5¼ x 7. 24636-1

OLD-TIME VIGNETTES IN FULL COLOR, Carol Belanger Grafton (ed.). Over 390 charming, often sentimental illustrations, selected from archives of Victorian graphics–pretty women posing, children playing, food, flowers, kittens and puppies, smiling cherubs, birds and butterflies, much more. All copyright-free. 48pp. 9¼ x 12¼. 27269-9

PERSPECTIVE FOR ARTISTS, Rex Vicat Cole. Depth, perspective of sky and sea, shadows, much more, not usually covered. 391 diagrams, 81 reproductions of drawings and paintings. 279pp. 5⅜ x 8½. 22487-2

DRAWING THE LIVING FIGURE, Joseph Sheppard. Innovative approach to artistic anatomy focuses on specifics of surface anatomy, rather than muscles and bones. Over 170 drawings of live models in front, back and side views, and in widely varying poses. Accompanying diagrams. 177 illustrations. Introduction. Index. 144pp. 8⅜ x11¼. 26723-7

GOTHIC AND OLD ENGLISH ALPHABETS: 100 Complete Fonts, Dan X. Solo. Add power, elegance to posters, signs, other graphics with 100 stunning copyright-free alphabets. Blackstone, Dolbey, Germania, 97 more–including many lower-case, numerals, punctuation marks. 104pp. 8⅛ x 11. 24695-7

HOW TO DO BEADWORK, Mary White. Fundamental book on craft from simple projects to five-bead chains and woven works. 106 illustrations. 142pp. 5⅜ x 8. 20697-1

THE BOOK OF WOOD CARVING, Charles Marshall Sayers. Finest book for beginners discusses fundamentals and offers 34 designs. "Absolutely first rate . . . well thought out and well executed."–E. J. Tangerman. 118pp. 7¾ x 10⅝. 23654-4

ILLUSTRATED CATALOG OF CIVIL WAR MILITARY GOODS: Union Army Weapons, Insignia, Uniform Accessories, and Other Equipment, Schuyler, Hartley, and Graham. Rare, profusely illustrated 1846 catalog includes Union Army uniform and dress regulations, arms and ammunition, coats, insignia, flags, swords, rifles, etc. 226 illustrations. 160pp. 9 x 12. 24939-5

WOMEN'S FASHIONS OF THE EARLY 1900s: An Unabridged Republication of "New York Fashions, 1909," National Cloak & Suit Co. Rare catalog of mail-order fashions documents women's and children's clothing styles shortly after the turn of the century. Captions offer full descriptions, prices. Invaluable resource for fashion, costume historians. Approximately 725 illustrations. 128pp. 8⅜ x 11¼. 27276-1

THE 1912 AND 1915 GUSTAV STICKLEY FURNITURE CATALOGS, Gustav Stickley. With over 200 detailed illustrations and descriptions, these two catalogs are essential reading and reference materials and identification guides for Stickley furniture. Captions cite materials, dimensions and prices. 112pp. 6½ x 9¼. 26676-1

EARLY AMERICAN LOCOMOTIVES, John H. White, Jr. Finest locomotive engravings from early 19th century: historical (1804–74), main-line (after 1870), special, foreign, etc. 147 plates. 142pp. 11⅜ x 8¼. 22772-3

THE TALL SHIPS OF TODAY IN PHOTOGRAPHS, Frank O. Braynard. Lavishly illustrated tribute to nearly 100 majestic contemporary sailing vessels: Amerigo Vespucci, Clearwater, Constitution, Eagle, Mayflower, Sea Cloud, Victory, many more. Authoritative captions provide statistics, background on each ship. 190 black-and-white photographs and illustrations. Introduction. 128pp. 8⅞ x 11¾. 27163-3

LITTLE BOOK OF EARLY AMERICAN CRAFTS AND TRADES, Peter Stockham (ed.). 1807 children's book explains crafts and trades: baker, hatter, cooper, potter, and many others. 23 copperplate illustrations. 140pp. 4⅝ x 6. 23336-7

VICTORIAN FASHIONS AND COSTUMES FROM HARPER'S BAZAR, 1867–1898, Stella Blum (ed.). Day costumes, evening wear, sports clothes, shoes, hats, other accessories in over 1,000 detailed engravings. 320pp. 9⅜ x 12¼. 22990-4

GUSTAV STICKLEY, THE CRAFTSMAN, Mary Ann Smith. Superb study surveys broad scope of Stickley's achievement, especially in architecture. Design philosophy, rise and fall of the Craftsman empire, descriptions and floor plans for many Craftsman houses, more. 86 black-and-white halftones. 31 line illustrations. Introduction 208pp. 6½ x 9¼. 27210-9

THE LONG ISLAND RAIL ROAD IN EARLY PHOTOGRAPHS, Ron Ziel. Over 220 rare photos, informative text document origin (1844) and development of rail service on Long Island. Vintage views of early trains, locomotives, stations, passengers, crews, much more. Captions. 8⅞ x 11¾. 26301-0

VOYAGE OF THE LIBERDADE, Joshua Slocum. Great 19th-century mariner's thrilling, first-hand account of the wreck of his ship off South America, the 35-foot boat he built from the wreckage, and its remarkable voyage home. 128pp. 5⅜ x 8½. 40022-0

TEN BOOKS ON ARCHITECTURE, Vitruvius. The most important book ever written on architecture. Early Roman aesthetics, technology, classical orders, site selection, all other aspects. Morgan translation. 331pp. 5⅜ x 8½. 20645-9

THE HUMAN FIGURE IN MOTION, Eadweard Muybridge. More than 4,500 stopped-action photos, in action series, showing undraped men, women, children jumping, lying down, throwing, sitting, wrestling, carrying, etc. 390pp. 7⅞ x 10⅝. 20204-6 Clothbd.

TREES OF THE EASTERN AND CENTRAL UNITED STATES AND CANADA, William M. Harlow. Best one-volume guide to 140 trees. Full descriptions, woodlore, range, etc. Over 600 illustrations. Handy size. 288pp. 4½ x 6⅜. 20395-6

SONGS OF WESTERN BIRDS, Dr. Donald J. Borror. Complete song and call repertoire of 60 western species, including flycatchers, juncoes, cactus wrens, many more–includes fully illustrated booklet. Cassette and manual 99913-0

GROWING AND USING HERBS AND SPICES, Milo Miloradovich. Versatile handbook provides all the information needed for cultivation and use of all the herbs and spices available in North America. 4 illustrations. Index. Glossary. 236pp. 5⅜ x 8½. 25058-X

BIG BOOK OF MAZES AND LABYRINTHS, Walter Shepherd. 50 mazes and labyrinths in all–classical, solid, ripple, and more–in one great volume. Perfect inexpensive puzzler for clever youngsters. Full solutions. 112pp. 8⅛ x 11. 22951-3

PIANO TUNING, J. Cree Fischer. Clearest, best book for beginner, amateur. Simple repairs, raising dropped notes, tuning by easy method of flattened fifths. No previous skills needed. 4 illustrations. 201pp. 5⅜ x 8½. 23267-0

HINTS TO SINGERS, Lillian Nordica. Selecting the right teacher, developing confidence, overcoming stage fright, and many other important skills receive thoughtful discussion in this indispensible guide, written by a world-famous diva of four decades' experience. 96pp. 5⅜ x 8½. 40094-8

THE COMPLETE NONSENSE OF EDWARD LEAR, Edward Lear. All nonsense limericks, zany alphabets, Owl and Pussycat, songs, nonsense botany, etc., illustrated by Lear. Total of 320pp. 5⅜ x 8½. (Available in U.S. only.) 20167-8

VICTORIAN PARLOUR POETRY: An Annotated Anthology, Michael R. Turner. 117 gems by Longfellow, Tennyson, Browning, many lesser-known poets. "The Village Blacksmith," "Curfew Must Not Ring Tonight," "Only a Baby Small," dozens more, often difficult to find elsewhere. Index of poets, titles, first lines. xxiii + 325pp. 5⅝ x 8¼. 27044-0

DUBLINERS, James Joyce. Fifteen stories offer vivid, tightly focused observations of the lives of Dublin's poorer classes. At least one, "The Dead," is considered a masterpiece. Reprinted complete and unabridged from standard edition. 160pp. 5$\frac{3}{16}$ x 8¼. 26870-5

GREAT WEIRD TALES: 14 Stories by Lovecraft, Blackwood, Machen and Others, S. T. Joshi (ed.). 14 spellbinding tales, including "The Sin Eater," by Fiona McLeod, "The Eye Above the Mantel," by Frank Belknap Long, as well as renowned works by R. H. Barlow, Lord Dunsany, Arthur Machen, W. C. Morrow and eight other masters of the genre. 256pp. 5⅜ x 8½. (Available in U.S. only.) 40436-6

THE BOOK OF THE SACRED MAGIC OF ABRAMELIN THE MAGE, translated by S. MacGregor Mathers. Medieval manuscript of ceremonial magic. Basic document in Aleister Crowley, Golden Dawn groups. 268pp. 5⅜ x 8½. 23211-5

NEW RUSSIAN-ENGLISH AND ENGLISH-RUSSIAN DICTIONARY, M. A. O'Brien. This is a remarkably handy Russian dictionary, containing a surprising amount of information, including over 70,000 entries. 366pp. 4½ x 6⅛. 20208-9

HISTORIC HOMES OF THE AMERICAN PRESIDENTS, Second, Revised Edition, Irvin Haas. A traveler's guide to American Presidential homes, most open to the public, depicting and describing homes occupied by every American President from George Washington to George Bush. With visiting hours, admission charges, travel routes. 175 photographs. Index. 160pp. 8¼ x 11. 26751-2

NEW YORK IN THE FORTIES, Andreas Feininger. 162 brilliant photographs by the well-known photographer, formerly with *Life* magazine. Commuters, shoppers, Times Square at night, much else from city at its peak. Captions by John von Hartz. 181pp. 9¼ x 10¾. 23585-8

INDIAN SIGN LANGUAGE, William Tomkins. Over 525 signs developed by Sioux and other tribes. Written instructions and diagrams. Also 290 pictographs. 111pp. 6⅛ x 9¼. 22029-X

PHOTOGRAPHIC SKETCHBOOK OF THE CIVIL WAR, Alexander Gardner. 100 photos taken on field during the Civil War. Famous shots of Manassas Harper's Ferry, Lincoln, Richmond, slave pens, etc. 244pp. 10⅝ x 8¼. 22731-6

FIVE ACRES AND INDEPENDENCE, Maurice G. Kains. Great back-to-the-land classic explains basics of self-sufficient farming. The one book to get. 95 illustrations. 397pp. 5⅜ x 8½. 20974-1

SONGS OF EASTERN BIRDS, Dr. Donald J. Borror. Songs and calls of 60 species most common to eastern U.S.: warblers, woodpeckers, flycatchers, thrushes, larks, many more in high-quality recording. Cassette and manual 99912-2

A MODERN HERBAL, Margaret Grieve. Much the fullest, most exact, most useful compilation of herbal material. Gigantic alphabetical encyclopedia, from aconite to zedoary, gives botanical information, medical properties, folklore, economic uses, much else. Indispensable to serious reader. 161 illustrations. 888pp. 6½ x 9¼. 2-vol. set. (Available in U.S. only.) Vol. I: 22798-7
Vol. II: 22799-5

HIDDEN TREASURE MAZE BOOK, Dave Phillips. Solve 34 challenging mazes accompanied by heroic tales of adventure. Evil dragons, people-eating plants, bloodthirsty giants, many more dangerous adversaries lurk at every twist and turn. 34 mazes, stories, solutions. 48pp. 8¼ x 11. 24566-7

LETTERS OF W. A. MOZART, Wolfgang A. Mozart. Remarkable letters show bawdy wit, humor, imagination, musical insights, contemporary musical world; includes some letters from Leopold Mozart. 276pp. 5⅜ x 8½. 22859-2

BASIC PRINCIPLES OF CLASSICAL BALLET, Agrippina Vaganova. Great Russian theoretician, teacher explains methods for teaching classical ballet. 118 illustrations. 175pp. 5⅜ x 8½. 22036-2

THE JUMPING FROG, Mark Twain. Revenge edition. The original story of The Celebrated Jumping Frog of Calaveras County, a hapless French translation, and Twain's hilarious "retranslation" from the French. 12 illustrations. 66pp. 5⅜ x 8½.
22686-7

BEST REMEMBERED POEMS, Martin Gardner (ed.). The 126 poems in this superb collection of 19th- and 20th-century British and American verse range from Shelley's "To a Skylark" to the impassioned "Renascence" of Edna St. Vincent Millay and to Edward Lear's whimsical "The Owl and the Pussycat." 224pp. 5⅜ x 8½.
27165-X

COMPLETE SONNETS, William Shakespeare. Over 150 exquisite poems deal with love, friendship, the tyranny of time, beauty's evanescence, death and other themes in language of remarkable power, precision and beauty. Glossary of archaic terms. 80pp. 5³⁄₁₆ x 8¼. 26686-9

THE BATTLES THAT CHANGED HISTORY, Fletcher Pratt. Eminent historian profiles 16 crucial conflicts, ancient to modern, that changed the course of civilization. 352pp. 5⅜ x 8½. 41129-X

THE WIT AND HUMOR OF OSCAR WILDE, Alvin Redman (ed.). More than 1,000 ripostes, paradoxes, wisecracks: Work is the curse of the drinking classes; I can resist everything except temptation; etc. 258pp. 5⅜ x 8½. 20602-5

SHAKESPEARE LEXICON AND QUOTATION DICTIONARY, Alexander Schmidt. Full definitions, locations, shades of meaning in every word in plays and poems. More than 50,000 exact quotations. 1,485pp. 6½ x 9¼. 2-vol. set.

Vol. 1: 22726-X
Vol. 2: 22727-8

SELECTED POEMS, Emily Dickinson. Over 100 best-known, best-loved poems by one of America's foremost poets, reprinted from authoritative early editions. No comparable edition at this price. Index of first lines. 64pp. 5³⁄₁₆ x 8¼. 26466-1

THE INSIDIOUS DR. FU-MANCHU, Sax Rohmer. The first of the popular mystery series introduces a pair of English detectives to their archnemesis, the diabolical Dr. Fu-Manchu. Flavorful atmosphere, fast-paced action, and colorful characters enliven this classic of the genre. 208pp. 5³⁄₁₆ x 8¼. 29898-1

THE MALLEUS MALEFICARUM OF KRAMER AND SPRENGER, translated by Montague Summers. Full text of most important witchhunter's "bible," used by both Catholics and Protestants. 278pp. 6⅝ x 10. 22802-9

SPANISH STORIES/CUENTOS ESPAÑOLES: A Dual-Language Book, Angel Flores (ed.). Unique format offers 13 great stories in Spanish by Cervantes, Borges, others. Faithful English translations on facing pages. 352pp. 5⅜ x 8½. 25399-6

GARDEN CITY, LONG ISLAND, IN EARLY PHOTOGRAPHS, 1869–1919, Mildred H. Smith. Handsome treasury of 118 vintage pictures, accompanied by carefully researched captions, document the Garden City Hotel fire (1899), the Vanderbilt Cup Race (1908), the first airmail flight departing from the Nassau Boulevard Aerodrome (1911), and much more. 96pp. 8⅞ x 11¾. 40669-5

OLD QUEENS, N.Y., IN EARLY PHOTOGRAPHS, Vincent F. Seyfried and William Asadorian. Over 160 rare photographs of Maspeth, Jamaica, Jackson Heights, and other areas. Vintage views of DeWitt Clinton mansion, 1939 World's Fair and more. Captions. 192pp. 8⅞ x 11. 26358-4

CAPTURED BY THE INDIANS: 15 Firsthand Accounts, 1750-1870, Frederick Drimmer. Astounding true historical accounts of grisly torture, bloody conflicts, relentless pursuits, miraculous escapes and more, by people who lived to tell the tale. 384pp. 5⅜ x 8½. 24901-8

THE WORLD'S GREAT SPEECHES (Fourth Enlarged Edition), Lewis Copeland, Lawrence W. Lamm, and Stephen J. McKenna. Nearly 300 speeches provide public speakers with a wealth of updated quotes and inspiration–from Pericles' funeral oration and William Jennings Bryan's "Cross of Gold Speech" to Malcolm X's powerful words on the Black Revolution and Earl of Spenser's tribute to his sister, Diana, Princess of Wales. 944pp. 5⅜ x 8⅜. 40903-1

THE BOOK OF THE SWORD, Sir Richard F. Burton. Great Victorian scholar/adventurer's eloquent, erudite history of the "queen of weapons"–from prehistory to early Roman Empire. Evolution and development of early swords, variations (sabre, broadsword, cutlass, scimitar, etc.), much more. 336pp. 6⅛ x 9¼. 25434-8

AUTOBIOGRAPHY: The Story of My Experiments with Truth, Mohandas K. Gandhi. Boyhood, legal studies, purification, the growth of the Satyagraha (nonviolent protest) movement. Critical, inspiring work of the man responsible for the freedom of India. 480pp. 5⅜ x 8½. (Available in U.S. only.) 24593-4

CELTIC MYTHS AND LEGENDS, T. W. Rolleston. Masterful retelling of Irish and Welsh stories and tales. Cuchulain, King Arthur, Deirdre, the Grail, many more. First paperback edition. 58 full-page illustrations. 512pp. 5⅜ x 8½. 26507-2

THE PRINCIPLES OF PSYCHOLOGY, William James. Famous long course complete, unabridged. Stream of thought, time perception, memory, experimental methods; great work decades ahead of its time. 94 figures. 1,391pp. 5⅜ x 8½. 2-vol. set. Vol. I: 20381-6 Vol. II: 20382-4

THE WORLD AS WILL AND REPRESENTATION, Arthur Schopenhauer. Definitive English translation of Schopenhauer's life work, correcting more than 1,000 errors, omissions in earlier translations. Translated by E. F. J. Payne. Total of 1,269pp. 5⅜ x 8½. 2-vol. set. Vol. 1: 21761-2 Vol. 2: 21762-0

MAGIC AND MYSTERY IN TIBET, Madame Alexandra David-Neel. Experiences among lamas, magicians, sages, sorcerers, Bonpa wizards. A true psychic discovery. 32 illustrations. 321pp. 5⅜ x 8½. (Available in U.S. only.) 22682-4

THE EGYPTIAN BOOK OF THE DEAD, E. A. Wallis Budge. Complete reproduction of Ani's papyrus, finest ever found. Full hieroglyphic text, interlinear transliteration, word-for-word translation, smooth translation. 533pp. 6½ x 9¼. 21866-X

MATHEMATICS FOR THE NONMATHEMATICIAN, Morris Kline. Detailed, college-level treatment of mathematics in cultural and historical context, with numerous exercises. Recommended Reading Lists. Tables. Numerous figures. 641pp. 5⅜ x 8½. 24823-2

PROBABILISTIC METHODS IN THE THEORY OF STRUCTURES, Isaac Elishakoff. Well-written introduction covers the elements of the theory of probability from two or more random variables, the reliability of such multivariable structures, the theory of random function, Monte Carlo methods of treating problems incapable of exact solution, and more. Examples. 502pp. 5⅜ x 8½. 40691-1

THE RIME OF THE ANCIENT MARINER, Gustave Doré, S. T. Coleridge. Doré's finest work; 34 plates capture moods, subtleties of poem. Flawless full-size reproductions printed on facing pages with authoritative text of poem. "Beautiful. Simply beautiful."–*Publisher's Weekly*. 77pp. 9¼ x 12. 22305-1

NORTH AMERICAN INDIAN DESIGNS FOR ARTISTS AND CRAFTSPEOPLE, Eva Wilson. Over 360 authentic copyright-free designs adapted from Navajo blankets, Hopi pottery, Sioux buffalo hides, more. Geometrics, symbolic figures, plant and animal motifs, etc. 128pp. 8⅜ x 11. (Not for sale in the United Kingdom.) 25341-4

SCULPTURE: Principles and Practice, Louis Slobodkin. Step-by-step approach to clay, plaster, metals, stone; classical and modern. 253 drawings, photos. 255pp. 8⅛ x 11. 22960-2

THE INFLUENCE OF SEA POWER UPON HISTORY, 1660–1783, A. T. Mahan. Influential classic of naval history and tactics still used as text in war colleges. First paperback edition. 4 maps. 24 battle plans. 640pp. 5⅜ x 8½. 25509-3

THE STORY OF THE TITANIC AS TOLD BY ITS SURVIVORS, Jack Winocour (ed.). What it was really like. Panic, despair, shocking inefficiency, and a little heroism. More thrilling than any fictional account. 26 illustrations. 320pp. 5⅜ x 8½. 20610-6

FAIRY AND FOLK TALES OF THE IRISH PEASANTRY, William Butler Yeats (ed.). Treasury of 64 tales from the twilight world of Celtic myth and legend: "The Soul Cages," "The Kildare Pooka," "King O'Toole and his Goose," many more. Introduction and Notes by W. B. Yeats. 352pp. 5⅜ x 8½. 26941-8

BUDDHIST MAHAYANA TEXTS, E. B. Cowell and others (eds.). Superb, accurate translations of basic documents in Mahayana Buddhism, highly important in history of religions. The Buddha-karita of Asvaghosha, Larger Sukhavativyuha, more. 448pp. 5⅜ x 8½. 25552-2

ONE TWO THREE . . . INFINITY: Facts and Speculations of Science, George Gamow. Great physicist's fascinating, readable overview of contemporary science: number theory, relativity, fourth dimension, entropy, genes, atomic structure, much more. 128 illustrations. Index. 352pp. 5⅜ x 8½. 25664-2

EXPERIMENTATION AND MEASUREMENT, W. J. Youden. Introductory manual explains laws of measurement in simple terms and offers tips for achieving accuracy and minimizing errors. Mathematics of measurement, use of instruments, experimenting with machines. 1994 edition. Foreword. Preface. Introduction. Epilogue. Selected Readings. Glossary. Index. Tables and figures. 128pp. 5⅜ x 8½. 40451-X

DALÍ ON MODERN ART: The Cuckolds of Antiquated Modern Art, Salvador Dalí. Influential painter skewers modern art and its practitioners. Outrageous evaluations of Picasso, Cézanne, Turner, more. 15 renderings of paintings discussed. 44 calligraphic decorations by Dalí. 96pp. 5⅜ x 8½. (Available in U.S. only.) 29220-7

ANTIQUE PLAYING CARDS: A Pictorial History, Henry René D'Allemagne. Over 900 elaborate, decorative images from rare playing cards (14th–20th centuries): Bacchus, death, dancing dogs, hunting scenes, royal coats of arms, players cheating, much more. 96pp. 9¼ x 12¼. 29265-7

MAKING FURNITURE MASTERPIECES: 30 Projects with Measured Drawings, Franklin H. Gottshall. Step-by-step instructions, illustrations for constructing handsome, useful pieces, among them a Sheraton desk, Chippendale chair, Spanish desk, Queen Anne table and a William and Mary dressing mirror. 224pp. 8⅛ x 11¼. 29338-6

THE FOSSIL BOOK: A Record of Prehistoric Life, Patricia V. Rich et al. Profusely illustrated definitive guide covers everything from single-celled organisms and dinosaurs to birds and mammals and the interplay between climate and man. Over 1,500 illustrations. 760pp. 7½ x 10⅛. 29371-8

Paperbound unless otherwise indicated. Available at your book dealer, online at **www.doverpublications.com**, or by writing to Dept. GI, Dover Publications, Inc., 31 East 2nd Street, Mineola, NY 11501. For current price information or for free catalogues (please indicate field of interest), write to Dover Publications or log on to **www.doverpublications.com** and see every Dover book in print. Dover publishes more than 500 books each year on science, elementary and advanced mathematics, biology, music, art, literary history, social sciences, and other areas.